From *Suck* to Success

A GUIDE FOR EXTRAORDINARY ENTREPRENEURSHIP

By Todd Palmer

ExtraordinaryAdvisors.com

•••

To Jane,
Thank you for being an Extraordinary
leader.
Best Regards,
(signature) Todd Palmer
2021

From Suck to Success:
A Guide for Extraordinary Entrepreneurship
© 2021 Todd Palmer

Published by Tulip Media Group

ASIN B08VNNPMWM
ISBN 978-0-578-85644-5

Printed in the United States of America.

Praise for
From Suck to Success

In 2020, the business world was rocked by COVID-19. Our business was reeling, too. Todd Palmer reached out to fellow members of the Entrepreneurs' Organization to generously offer his powerful history of experiences and expertise on navigating a crash and recovery. I connected with Todd via Zoom, Australia to the US. We had never met, but we instantly connected on the common synergy of business. Understanding the intense journey of Todd's success refreshed my perspective and confidence to surge forward in unprecedented times. A reminder that we are not alone. Over the years, Todd has filled his big-business toolbox with experiences and learning to share in abundance. Todd also reminded me that I had the answers—I just needed to look deeper. Quality conversation sparks ideas—get your real world ideas from Todd's extraordinary entrepreneurship and surge forward.
— Christine Green, cofounder of Food Strategy, Southern Cross Food Equipment, Coldroom Shelving, and Restaurant Bookkeepers Australia

Building a successful business is anything but linear and predictable. Having an experienced, talented guide to help navigate the ups and downs of business is critical to success. Todd Palmer has been such a guide for hundreds of business owners who willingly invested in his direction and support. In *From Suck to Success*, Todd is bringing years of experience directly to you. This is a must read for business builders.
— Brian Brault, cochair, Entrepreneurial Masters Program, and former chairman, Entrepreneurs' Organization

Todd has helped several leaders navigate the ups and downs of building a business. Todd's insights are typically only shared with his clients; however, in *From Suck to Success*, he is now sharing his experience and guidance with you. I have benefited greatly from his guidance and know that it will be a worthwhile investment of your time.

— Phil Rankin, president and founder, Triad Capital Group

As entrepreneurs, it's easy for us to say what we want out of a business. What's unique about Todd's message is the equal importance he places on understanding what we don't want. So, if you're feeling stuck, understand that breakthroughs come when you finally stop tolerating those things you never wanted. Luckily, Todd's got a plan to get you unstuck, and you're already holding it in your hand.

— Travis Scott Luther, founder of the Queen Anne Pillow Company

What I have learned from Todd Palmer about how to navigate natural business fluctuations is priceless. As a coach, he is more than worth the investment, for profitability and peace of mind. In this book, he hacked his own coaching techniques; you get his applicable wisdom without the coaching price tag.

— Jacki Smith, founder, Coventry Creations

Todd has helped me for the past several years to navigate the changing landscape of business. He has coached me on how to address the good and the bad and the ups and the downs. Todd's insight into how the journey works is invaluable. Now Todd is sharing his knowledge in *From Suck to Success* with everyone.

— Scott Jackson, president, Alta Vista Technology

With more than twenty-five years of experience, Todd Palmer has helped hundreds of entrepreneurs grow and scale their businesses. In this book, Todd shares his lessons as a business leader on how to navigate the challenging process to success with intention and determination.

— Patrick Fehring, president and CEO, Level One Bank

Todd is a longtime friend who has a passion for people and business. He is a successful coach because he takes the time to ask lots of questions and he listens. Todd has lived the journey of owning a business and understands that success is not linear. This book is a culmination of many of Todd's experiences, and his vulnerability and insight shine in it.
— **Scott A. Eisenberg, partner and cofounder, Amherst Partners**

Todd Palmer knows business and knows that it is not a straight line. With his humor and candid stories, he demonstrates that it can be done, but it is not a linear process. Typically, people invest a lot of money to gain Todd's wisdom, but he is opening it up in his new book for everyone to benefit!
— **Erin K. Arnold, president, NextStep Networking**

Todd Palmer is an entrepreneur, innovator, coach, and educator. He has helped hundreds of business owners navigate the ups and downs of building a business. Todd has an innate ability to pinpoint deficiencies, create transparency, and coach organizations towards finding success. Typically, those business owners make a capital investment for Todd's direction and support. With *From Suck to Success*, Todd is now opening up his vast knowledge to the world. We are all fortunate to have the opportunity to learn from such a tremendous business mind.
— **Royce Neubauer, CEO, SFL Companies**

Todd Palmer has and continues to be an inspiration in navigating the roller-coaster ride of owning a business. In true entrepreneurial fashion, he is taking it one step further by launching his book, *From Suck to Success*! Todd is opening up his wealth of knowledge and expertise so people all over the world can benefit and pivot in their business and in life. This book will be a game changer to those looking for direction, expert leadership, and support.
— **Kate Holden, owner, De Luca Fine Wines and Flaunt Boutique**

I've known a lot of coaches. Todd Palmer is not like any coach I have ever met. Like the late John Wooden, Todd is always coaching, and he brings that passion for helping others along with his real-life experience to his latest book, *From Suck to Success*. His approach of having leaders work from the inside out, to make complicated things simple, is truly life changing. If you want to create a life by design or grow and scale a company, *From Suck to Success* is a must read.

— **Deb Gabor, CEO, Sol Marketing, and best-selling author of *Branding Is Sex***

From Suck to Success works! Todd is an amazing coach, and I've been fortunate to work with him personally. The principles in this book are gems, and we have used all of them to pivot and grow our mind-set. I have put in so much work to move away and achieve a growth mind-set. One of the big things we tackled was banishing the Itty Bitty Shitty Committee. And yes, I emphasize the Shitty part. I've gone from Imposter to "I suck" and everything in between, and we have worked diligently to banish those jokers. They don't serve a bit of a purpose, and I was finally able to discern good from evil and figure out exactly when to relegate the Itty Bitty Shitty Committee to the back seat. *From Suck to Success* can truly help you create an amazing life.

—**Eric Samdahl, fractional CEO/COO and founder, GHSD Group**

Dedication

To my son, Tyler.

Being your dad has been the absolute highlight of my life. I love you.

Contents

Foreword_____13

Extraordinary_____19

Preface_____23

Introduction: The Thin Line Between Suck and Success____29

Part 1: Taking Inventory

Chapter 1: Figure Out Your Mind-Set First_____45

Chapter 2: Learning To Be Authentic, Transparent,
and Vulnerable_____69

Chapter 3: Setting An Intention, Not An Expectation_____93

Chapter 4: The E-4 Process That Can Improve Your
Mind-Set, Leadership, And Results_____113

Part 2: Taking Action

Chapter 5: Looping Toward Success_____129

Chapter 6: Empowering Yourself With People_____157

Chapter 7: Leadership Strategies For The Worst Of Times__177

Chapter 8: Designing Your Ultimate Life_____199

Conclusion And Next Steps_____209

Acknowledgments_____217

Epilogue_____221

Reference_____225

About The Author_____231

Foreword

By Daniel Friedland, MD

As a coach, I have special moments when I feel deeply moved and inspired by my clients. This is such a moment. I've been blessed to be Todd's coach since 2014 and honored to have a front-row seat to share in this significant milestone of his journey—as he describes it in his unique voice—*From Suck to Success.*

Much of the culmination of Todd's success is not only in writing this book but is also deeply reflected in his dedication to his son, Tyler: "Being your dad has been the absolute highlight of my life. I love you."

With Todd's permission, I can share with you why this dedication is so meaningful. When Todd began his coaching with me, I asked him what would represent the greatest success as a result of our journey together. He shared with me how his deepest pain was feeling estranged and disconnected from Tyler and just how much this "sucked." "Success" would be their reconnecting in an authentic and loving relationship together.

In the early years, this became a major part of our work together, a purposeful curriculum in learning how to open his heart with greater self-compassion to make space for vulnerability through which greater love and compassion flows. To make this happen, Todd set a steady intention and took courageous action. Over the months, it was awe inspiring to watch how through his small and then larger conversations with Tyler, Todd was able to find the success he was seeking and ultimately express to his son, "I'm proud of the man you've become! I love you."

Much of the foundational work Todd and I have done together has been anchored in my book, *Leading Well from Within: A Neuroscience and Mindfulness-Based Framework for Conscious Leadership.*

Whether you are an entrepreneur, parent, healer, coach, or friend, leadership is an act of influence. Conscious leadership cultivates the awareness and ability to lead from your highest self where you can experience greater joy, success, and significance that comes from being a positive influence in the lives of others.

The arc of this growth involves engaging key skills and practices to shift from a reactive mind-set, where the threat of stress and self-doubt trigger fight-or-flight reactions that often impede the ability to connect or perform well, to a creative mind-set, where we are more self-aware, compassionate, and innovative and where our lives thrive with greater meaning, significance, and fulfillment. Furthermore, the creative mind-set has been shown to result in higher levels of business performance as it relates to sales and revenue growth, market share, profitability, quality of products and services, new product development, and overall performance.[1]

During the years that Todd and I have been working together, we've been integrating this learning and growth by leveraging the active learning cycle (adapted from the work of David Kolb around Experiential Learning[2]). As shown in the figure below, this process has three components:

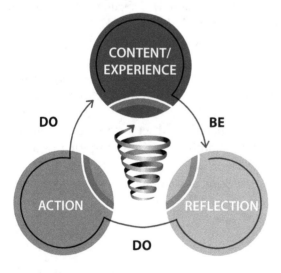

1. Content or experience
2. Reflection
3. Action

It was inspiring to watch how Todd fully invested himself in this cycle with his deeply meaningful goal to reconnect with Tyler. For example, after Todd expressed this purpose, we focused on the content and experiences around self-compassion. He reflected on how this could diminish some of the reactivity he had been feeling and open his heart to express greater compassion for Tyler. This enabled him to engage a creative mind-set and more clearly identify the specific actions that would serve him best in making significant progress towards his purposeful goal.

This cycle is iterative. The series of actions Todd took led to new reflections and new actions that led to new experiences in an upward spiral of learning and growth.

In many ways, the success of coaching lies more in the hands of the clients than the coaches. This success relates to how deeply clients invest in their active learning cycle and essentially engage in their own self-coaching. The key ingredients—or "internal activation factors"—for success in self-coaching are ownership, openness, kindness, curiosity, presence, and ultimately being self-accountable for purpose-aligned actions.

It's been a joy to see how Todd has fully embraced these activation factors to engage in his self-coaching journey and claim his success. Beyond reconnecting with Tyler, he has leveraged this active learning cycle to achieve success in countless other ways, including his shift from his staffing business to his coaching business—where he connects even more deeply with his passion and purpose in making a meaningful difference in the lives of others through coaching—and with this book you now have in your hands.

Much of the power of *From Suck to Success* lies in how it engages you in your own self-coaching by engaging you in your own active learning cycle. Todd has written this life-changing book to make it easy and compelling for you to engage this cycle and succeed in multiple ways.

You'll notice that:

> The book is framed in two parts: Taking Inventory (i.e., Reflection) and Taking Action.

Each chapter summarizes its content with "Insights" and provides "Questions for Your Reflection" and suggests "Action Steps."

In Chapter 4—"The Four-Step Process That Can Improve Your Mind-Set, Leadership, and Results"—Todd engages you in iterative cycles of reflection and action to facilitate your success.

In this book, Todd will share with you the power of authenticity, transparency, and vulnerability in learning and growing to become a more effective person. He truly embodies these values. Todd walks his talk and speaks from the wisdom born of the personal transformation he's experienced in business and with a number of coaches.

Now it's time for you to benefit from what he has to share. Todd has a gift for making the complicated simple and more easily accessible with transformative insights to help you get unstuck or to get you where you want to go.

If you let Todd walk beside you as you read this book, invest in your self-coaching with reflection, and take action, you can look forward to what Todd promises in the final chapter: to ultimately live your extraordinary life, well lived!

Daniel Friedland, MD
CEO, SuperSmartHealth
San Diego, California
November 2020

Extraordinary

This book will help you lead an extraordinary life and build an extraordinary business.

Type "extraordinary" into a visual thesaurus and you'll see a constellation of superlatives, from "Olympian" and "special" to "singular" and "wonderworking."

It is my intention for you to be all of these, and more, by turning these pages. But you will need to work for your extraordinary life and your extraordinary business.

Because it's not extraordinary for a kid to get a C on a school project, or for an entrepreneur to make enough money to buy a car wash and a packet of Twizzlers after paying everybody else. Society has sanitized and homogenized the word "extraordinary" to the point where it's meaningless.

And I'm here to help bring that meaning back. I want to reclaim the word *extraordinary*.

When you live an extraordinary life, you define your own success.

When you live an extraordinary life, you have an iterative attitude to cope with failure.

When you live an extraordinary life, you realize extreme self-actualization.

And you are going to gain each of these by allowing me to help you build a self-fulfilling model of *what you really want.*

Climbers who find scaling mountains so fulfilling they'll suffer for it, and who will surround themselves with a tribe of people they know and trust, who aren't going to let them down? That's extraordinary.

> "In the willingness to fail, the extraordinary will often appear."
> —Anonymous

The Instagram shot of a guy in front of a yacht with three models? That's not extraordinary. That's not even his life.

Let's get back to you. You keep telling yourself you can be more. So what's holding you back?

This is not the time to dabble in things, to hire a coach just so you can tell your friends.

This is the time to double down for a singular life—an extraordinary life. Type "ordinary" into a visual thesaurus and you'll see words like "mundane," "run-of-the-mill," and "average."

Amazingly, some entrepreneurs who hire me as a coach seem to want to be average and mundane. They want an ordinary life, because they are not willing to make the extraordinary effort to be singular and special, and to work wonders with their life.

If you want an ordinary life, put this book down. Walk away.

The rest of you can join me on an extraordinary journey. Let's go.

Preface

In 2006, I never would have thought this book was possible as I sat on a curb in front of my longtime business in Farmington Hills, Michigan, bawling my eyes out.

What led to my sitting there that day still brings back a physical reaction when I think about it. My business, my baby, Diversified Industrial Staffing, was $600,000 in debt. I was sixty days away from completely running out of cash.

It was severe, a combination of poor decisions made by me, and clients filing bankruptcy to the tune of $219,000. The $600,000 in debt was tied to a business with $2.5 million in revenue, and razor-thin margins.

I had hired my brother, Greg, for professional business consultation. Greg had extensive expertise in the staffing industry and could look at my business objectively. And even in the first conversations I had with him, I noticed a significant improvement in my mind-set, which is something I desperately needed at the time. I couldn't think of anyone better to hire as my coach.

Even though I'd hired a business coach whom I trusted implicitly, I still felt completely alone, panicked, and paranoid as I sat on the curb that day. The complexity of my circumstances caused me to shut down. I had no idea how I had allowed myself to fall so deeply into debt. I no longer trusted my staff and definitely didn't trust myself. So on September 9, 2006, with my brother and coach, Greg, right by my side, I made difficult decision after difficult decision, starting with firing each and every employee. After letting everyone go, I walked out of my office, crumpled down on the curb, and cried for what felt like an eternity, but was probably more like a couple minutes.

As I sat there, I was filled with self-hatred and shame. I had just seriously considered filing for bankruptcy protection and shutting the business down completely. Instead, I decided I would attempt one last effort to build my business back up, only this time doing it differently. I was also dreading returning home to my fourteen-year-old son, Tyler. I became a single dad when he was only two years old. Since then, I'd taught Tyler to be a man of his word and to be honest with everyone he met. I'd taught him to honor his commitments no matter how hard it might be. Now I was faced with the thought of having to go home to tell him my business failed because I failed to do any of the things with Diversified Industrial Staffing that I tell other companies to do today. My 2006 mess has become my current message.

After my employees packed up their personal belongings, I met with Greg again. This time, we didn't talk numbers or business strategy. Our conversation focused solely on mind-set. He gave me thirty minutes to have what he called a "pity party." During those thirty minutes, I could say or do whatever I wanted. I could beat myself up. I could call myself a fool. I could wallow in sorrow. After thirty minutes, I had to pick myself up, dust myself off, and get to work on shifting my mind-set from a pity party to making progress in the right direction.

As the clock wound down and my pity party was ending, Greg gave me one simple instruction. "Get up and find something positive to do." No mind-set exercise. No affirmations. Nothing. Just get up and do something positive, such as calling my favorite clients or making some marketing calls to get new business. It was one of the more uncomfortable moments of my life. I had just finished calling myself things I wouldn't call my worst enemy. The last thing I was motivated to do was something positive. But I trusted him that if you "take action first, the motivation will follow."

Greg and I spent the next several days working to get me unstuck and moving in a better direction for rebuilding my business to become better.

During that time, we summarized five key business principles that would shape me into a better leader while rebuilding Diversified Industrial Staffing into a healthier, more profitable, and more stable company:

1. Do something positive every day.
2. Take care of yourself.
3. Focus on margin over revenue.
4. Have a daily huddle with your staff.
5. Practice financial transparency.

Those days, and the five key principles that came out of them, were the turning point of a new entrepreneurial career for me, and a new life that has landed me more fulfillment than I ever dreamed. Diversified Industrial Staffing came back bigger and stronger, and it was named to the prestigious *Inc. 5000* list of America's fastest growing companies six times in seven years. We paid off all of the $600,000 in debt by 2013. And because I built back Diversified Industrial Staffing in such a way that it didn't rely on me to do everything, I was able to build my own coaching and consulting practice to help business owners around the world avoid or dig themselves out of messes like the one I found myself in back in 2006.

I now feel as passionate about helping other business owners as I do about the work Diversified Industrial Staffing does to help skilled trade workers and employers find each other. And that's how this book came about. Since starting my coaching and consulting work, I've worked with countless entrepreneurs at various stages in their businesses.

Throughout that time, a pattern has emerged. Entrepreneurs are often just a few actions away from a meaningful pivot. Some actions lead to your business (and often your personal life) sucking—big time. That might not mean "sitting on a curb bawling your eyes out" sucking, but it will suck. You'll work too hard and make too little. You'll be anxious all the time. You'll never be able to physically or mentally escape the business. You'll build a house of cards, at best. Other actions will lead to your business (and often your personal life) becoming successful beyond your wildest dreams. You will work more *on* your business than in *it*. You will be able to trust your team, take vacations, and get your mind off your business when you're home.

Going from *Suck to Success* is really a matter of taking small but difficult actions to improve your mind-set, personal fulfillment, margins, and team building. If you have those pieces in place, everything else is really just a matter of detail. Throughout the rest of this book, I will share with you the lessons I learned and actions that helped me and other entrepreneurs go from *Suck to Success*—and for a fortunate few, avoid going too far into the "suck" direction altogether. I'll demonstrate how the lessons and strategies work in the real world by sharing real-life stories from my experience as well as from some of my coaching or consulting clients, with their blessing of course.

My goal is for you to use this book as a series of virtual coaching sessions with me. Don't be constrained by the traditional way we're taught to read books, from the beginning to the end without stopping. I share stories to entertain you and put the strategies I teach into context for you to help you see how they work in real life. But my goal isn't only to entertain you. It's to help you change your life. So, maybe you're more comfortable reading from the beginning to the end. That's fine. But *just* reading the book won't change your life. Applying the strategies to your life will.

If you want to sprint through the book one time like so many of us are used to doing, fine. But don't put the book away after that first read. Instead, turn back to the beginning, grab a pencil and paper, and treat the book like a workbook. Imagine you hired me to train you to apply the strategies to your business and your life. Schedule the time to apply the lessons in this book like you would schedule training or coaching sessions with me.

For example, you could break up the reading into hour-long sessions. During each of those sessions, work on a strategy with which you need help. Maybe you read for the first thirty minutes and then make an action plan and commitment for the rest of the time. Or maybe you work better by reading and outlining a strategy and commitment throughout the entire hour. Or maybe you choose one strategy at a time and work on it for a few sessions before moving on. Whatever you do, don't just put away the book and go back to your busy life. You, your team members, your family, and your business deserve to become extraordinary. I want that for you, too. And you can achieve it by putting to work the strategies I share in this book. Small steps over time will yield big results.

I wrote this book with the goal of making sure every business owner and corporate leader had simple tools to improve their business and life. It doesn't matter if you're just starting out or have been in business for decades, the strategies I share here can help. It doesn't matter if you are a mid-level leader in a large organization or a C-suite executive, the strategies can help. They're designed to strengthen the leader from within to help her lead with more conviction, confidence, and impact in business and in life.

You might not be ready to sit on that curb and have a good cry like I was. And you might not be overwhelmed by having way too much to do but way too little time like me, either. But if you want to become extraordinary—to define and take control of your future in business and in life—I want to help you.

As you read this book, consider me "your coach" and these pages "your own" adventure coaching session. These lessons have helped transform hundreds of businesses and the entrepreneurs who operate them. I know they can work for you, too. The best part is that, although some of the decisions you make or actions you must take will be difficult, they are not complicated. In fact, I've yet to meet an entrepreneur who couldn't do any of the things I suggest in this book. I've met some who *wouldn't*, but I have never met one who *couldn't*. So, if you're ready to make some difficult but life-altering changes to your business to avoid the suck and achieve success, I invite you to join me on a journey.

Introduction:

The Thin Line Between Suck And Success

Behind every successful business is a history of mistakes, failures, and embarrassing moments—some big and some small. Regardless of their size, these failures are essential to learning and to growing professionally and personally. My failure was big—and the best thing that could have happened to me.

When I started Diversified Industrial Staffing in 1997, I was young, in my mid-20s. I made a lot of assumptions regarding what the path of successful business ownership looked like. I thought it was a clear, rocket-ship ride from the bottom to the top.

I was clueless about the price entrepreneurs and their families pay to achieve their dreams. I had no idea of the toll the stress takes on our health, our relationships, and our financial stability. I never considered these facts—never even really knew they existed at the time. I didn't realize that starting a new business could be so all consuming, going far beyond the hours of nine to five. In other words, I didn't know what I didn't know.

I didn't know about fiduciary responsibilities: that the government and employees would get paid first and I would get paid last, if at all. I didn't realize that I had to know about legal issues, banking, financials, and employee issues. I didn't know that businesses had a higher failure rate than marriages.

I only saw that I could be my own boss and work the hours I wanted—and thought I would make boatloads of money. My plan was to be an overnight success.

My business and I both had some growing up to do and some growing pains to endure.

To backtrack just a bit further, before I started Diversified Industrial Staffing in 1997, I was a recently divorced single father. I had exclusive custody of my young son, Tyler. At the time, I was working as a sales representative for a temporary help company in metro Detroit. I had gotten into the staffing industry on the suggestion of my older brother, Greg, who ran a publicly held staffing firm with revenue in excess of $500 million.

And to paint the picture of my job at that time, I was supposed to make one hundred dials per day, cold-calling new businesses to see if they needed any temporary help personnel. These were the "olden days," before the widespread use of the internet, cloud technology, or anything like it. There were no Excel spreadsheets or software to support my daily efforts. It was a paper system. I started with the phone book, then I wrote out everything by hand.

I hated telephone cold-calling, so the one hundred dials were exquisitely painful. I took each rejection personally. I would have to psych myself up to push the buttons and call companies. It was nerve wracking, and an anxious feeling would tighten my chest.

Face-to-face knocking on doors wasn't any better. I had to go to industrial parks and collect business cards of those responsible for ordering temporary help so we could contact them to offer them candidates. But few wanted to give out that info. Receptionists were annoyed most of the time by my bothering them, which I could understand. I didn't like it much, either.

Sincerely wanting to improve, I bought and read several books on sales and cold-calling, thinking I might have been doing it wrong. But my anxiety was so high that I struggled to put any of the new knowledge into practice. I did discover that I was pretty good at the rest of the sales process once I could establish some face-to-face rapport. It was just building the initial rapport that I struggled with. But breaking the process into steps helped reduce my anxiety. Simplifying my thoughts did, too. I was good at fact-finding and asking questions, which really was a core part of the process. It was just the cold outreach itself that crippled me. On top of that, I couldn't really do much about it. I mentally broke out the transaction into cold outreach and relationship building, which helped. I simplified my thoughts, which also helped. But I still had to do all that cold outreach, and as an employee, there wasn't anything I could do about that.

I was disenchanted being an employee. I disagreed with my bosses' decisions. I was awful at corporate politics, and I did not see any sort of exciting future for my son and me. And for me, no excitement meant no production. I did not pretend to be enthusiastic about what I was doing. It was obvious to my bosses that I didn't care enough to try very hard on behalf of their company. I was a terrible employee.

Meanwhile, at age twenty-five, I kept reading about young entrepreneurs starting their own businesses and becoming immensely successful. I thought, "Time is running out; I need to do something different." I needed money. I needed to build a successful life for my young son and me, and I needed to do it right away while I was still young and had the energy.

One day, over lunch in the summer of 1997, I mentioned an idea I had for a staffing company to a former boss and friend named Mike. I shared with him my desire to start my own company and had a plan to do so with a budget of $140,000. He was intrigued by my plan, had some money to spare, and was interested in investing in me. He made clear that his investment was in me, not my plan. (I've learned that most investors look at the "who" behind the plan as one of the big three reasons to invest in anything.) He wasn't ready to commit to $140,000 that day, however, but he told me he believed in me and encouraged me to come up with a smaller plan to start.

The lesson I learned that day—that people invest in people, not business plans—was life changing. I assumed you needed a detailed business plan and a bank to get financing. In reality, without a founder who could demonstrate conviction, perseverance, trust, and fire, your business plan won't matter because most investors won't get that far. It also didn't hurt that I was good at presenting my case. After all, I had good rapport with Mike. He was far from a cold call.

Anything For A Buck

In September, I called Mike with a more realistic proposal: I could get started for $15,000 plus free office space at his existing business in Troy, Michigan. Bingo. On October 1, 1997, with a $15,000 loan from my silent partner and a 64-square-foot office in a back office, I opened my business, which I called "Diversified Staffing" at the time. My office was far from impressive, but it worked. I had a desk, a phone, my business card (with the title of president on it), letterhead, and the Yellow Pages to look for companies that needed temps. It was bootstrapped, to say the least.

Every morning, I would cold-call new businesses and former staffing customers from my previous company. Every afternoon, I'd see client prospects and job seekers. And every night, back home, I'd call candidates to see if they would go to work the next day. I taught myself QuickBooks and invoiced new clients each Tuesday night to keep cash coming in the door. There I was, a twenty-eight-year-old guy with a communications degree from Eastern Michigan University, representing all the departments of a "big company!" This was the true stuff of entrepreneurialism, or so I thought.

Little did I know, but I had chosen the most difficult route to start my business. Specifically, I had adopted a generalist model, trying to be everything to everyone. I didn't know any better, but Diversified Staffing might as well have been called "Anything for a Buck" Staffing. I simply followed the formula big companies in the staffing industry used, thinking that was my path to success. I quickly learned that it was more a path to stiff competition and pricing pressure. I also came right out of the gate competing against the big companies who had more resources, a deeper pool of candidates, and the ability to crush my margins to virtually nothing.

In the beginning, I kept my new business a secret from family and friends. I was so afraid of failing that I didn't tell anyone until the ninety-day mark. It was a real fear. Sure, I was thinking positively, but as Gabriele Oettingen writes of her studies in *Rethinking Positive Thinking*, "positive wishes, fantasies, wishes, and dreams detached from an assessment of past experience *[don't]* translate into motivation to act toward a more energized, engaged life."[3] My business "plan" wasn't much of a business plan. It was more of a dream or a wish backed up by some pretty unreasonable assumptions and lofty goals—completely detached from past experience (or reason).

Because I based much of my dreaming on what large staffing companies had built, I also defined success based on the size of my business. I believed I would only be successful if I did $20 million in staffing revenue, along with having multiple offices, a large staff, a corporate mentality, and an organizational chart to match. In my mind's eye, success was a large-scale everything.

In hindsight, this all seems irrational to me. Knowing what I know now, I cringe just typing this all out. But that was my reality. Instead of choosing a path of low competition, I competed against the big companies. And instead of measuring success based on impact and profit margin, I chose revenue targets and company size. I should have known I was on a fast track to financial ruin.

To make matters worse, I also tied myself psychologically to the company. If the company was successful, *I* was successful. We were one and the same. My self-worth was firmly attached to my business worth. You can imagine the highs and lows of this roller coaster. Every time I began to have a little self-doubt, it created fear, which is a self-fulfilling prophecy. I froze. I became stuck in my head. Fear became equivalent to inactivity. I was taking everything personally, so every cold call I made that didn't result in a sale crushed me.

Finally, as a final lesson in the "fast track to suck" business approach, I kept all of my stresses, questions, and mistakes to myself. I kept all my failures from my stakeholders. I carried the entire burden alone. I existed in a mental vacuum. This ate at my spirit and my drive. I endured this fear of failing and did my best to avoid it. Having all the answers was my mask and my way of not letting people see me sweat. I never showed vulnerability. I was the rugged individualist, driven to prove I could do it alone.

Needless to say, my definition of success and my plan to achieve it were both pretty screwed up at that point. I was working off of a definition of success as set by other people, as set by society. I was doing what I thought I should do to "make it," with bills and my ego chasing me every waking moment. I merged my self-worth with my business worth and kept everything to myself. What could possibly go wrong?

In Limbo

Stuck in the vicious entrepreneurial cycle, I limped along from 1997 to 2005 carrying every burden on my shoulders in a vicious pursuit of more and more business. We made money some years, lost money other years. But my focus was on landing "whales"—large-volume accounts that use a lot of temporary employees. Unfortunately, those "whales" only looked sexy when I could drop their company names at a party. In reality, those accounts squeezed every ounce of profit out of the work and demanded extended payment cycles. In other words, not only would my company make pennies on those whale accounts but I'd also have to wait months to get those pennies. I was essentially a bank to large companies, financing their temp workers for sixty days or longer. I was diverting payroll and payroll burden, making them my fiduciary responsibility. They had no incentive to pay me fast at all. They were getting a zero percent loan for at least sixty days on the money they had to pay me. That was my setup. That was the foundation of my business—targeting large companies, making pennies, and giving them zero percent interest loans on those pennies. That was the context in which I limped along from 1997 to 2005. Sounds promising, doesn't it?

My decisions during that period were consistently poor. It started in 1998 when I hired my first employee, my niece. It was a bad decision at that time to hire a family member. I realize that now. In the beginning, she did a very good job at sales and was successful in getting new business before becoming an account manager. However, she got in a car accident and wanted a six-month leave of absence to deal with some medical issues. While I wanted to support her, as a company of only two people and with a partner to pay back, I couldn't afford to give her a six-month leave of absence and had to let her go. That was tough.

The following year, I hired two experienced staffing industry veterans to take the business to the next level. They had more than twenty-five years of staffing industry knowledge, including growing offices organically. And they were expensive. But they paid immediate dividends by landing our second whale account in 2001, a large plating company that was running three full shifts per day. We set up a transportation company to get employees to work because the unemployment rate was so low. At this point, I had three offices running, eighteen internal employees, a transportation company to deliver people to work, and three large volume accounts. I was keeping the business running, but margins were tight.

By 2002, I'd made it past the fabled five-year mark, by which point 50 percent of entrepreneurs are said to fail. True success was within my reach—or so I thought.

In the first quarter of 2003, I quickly realized how fragile the foundation of Diversified Industrial Staffing was when the large plating company started stringing us along with payments and started to spread payments out beyond sixty days. My two experienced staffing guys told me this was common; such accounts always caught up on the money they owed. But by the summer, they were close to ninety days out on payments, and our bank was getting nervous. I was getting nervous, too, because I had personally guaranteed Diversified's credit lines and put my house up as collateral. But I was inexperienced with the warning signs of a distressed client and had trusted that everything would be paid off.

By the fall of 2003, the large plating company went belly up, and the $219,000 debt they owed to us wasn't worth the paper it was written on. Even worse, our bank called on the note I had personally guaranteed and threatened to shut us down and put us out of business. Luckily, with some ugly negotiations, we were able to hold the bank off and create a plan to pay off the debt. Additionally, the next year, we also landed our third whale, a Detroit-based pharmaceutical manufacturer. Within two years, the company represented 85 percent of our revenue. If that sounds risky, it's because it is. I learned that lesson the hard way when it decided to handle hiring in-house and stopped doing business with us in early 2006.

To say 1997–2006 was a roller coaster would be an understatement. I was stressed, overworked, and making way too little money. At the same time, I was getting bored and fed up with the world of temporary staffing. My services weren't appreciated. I was seen as a thankless commodity business driven by price, based on projects with no stable revenue stream, with low margins, slow receivables, and seemingly a new competitor every week. I *hated* to go to work—which is not a good thing when you own the place!

I wanted to start a different business, so I let go of the day-to-day operations of Diversified Industrial Staffing, turning them over to one of my highly paid executives, and started an employee leasing company to start focusing on more long-term relationships with companies. I convinced myself this direction would be more stable, with more long-term contracts, recurring revenue, and a broader appeal to any small business. Truthfully, I didn't give it much more thought than that. I was just looking for the next bright and shiny business opportunity that I thought would resolve one of my biggest frustrations with temporary work. Basically, it was a decision based on my ego and emotion. I hadn't really planned much better than when I started Diversified Industrial Staffing. But employee leasing sounded steadier to me, so I wrapped my emotional decision in flawed logic to justify it to myself.

During the first quarter of 2006, with my eye focused firmly on my new shiny object—my employee leasing business—I made one of the biggest mistakes an entrepreneur could make. Specifically, I took my eye completely off Diversified Industrial Staffing. I had a good-sized team who had been working with me for several years. And while I was intimately involved in operations to keep afloat during that time, when I started my employee leasing business, I left my other operations completely in the hands of my team. In other words, as flawed as my leadership was at the time, I completely removed a level of leadership they relied on so I could chase my new pet project.

At first, it paid off. The whale account was still active, and we were adding new, smaller accounts regularly. I thought I had the right team in place, and I praised myself for being such a good leader to train them and let them do their thing. I thought I had "figured it out." But then I made the grave mistake of completely taking my eye off the ball and creating a senior leadership void by leaving to start my new employee leasing business.

Taking The Speed Lane To Suck

As the calendar flipped to April 2006, so did our good fortune. We started losing money—a lot of money—and our fragile foundation became completely exposed. From April to September, we lost more than $240,000. Combine this with the previously bankrupted $219,000, and we were quickly approaching $600,000 in debt. It was my fault, too. I should have been on top of the business. I should have been more involved. I should not have trusted my team to correct the ship's course. They were trained in running the day-to-day operations but were not qualified to course correct or make big-picture decisions for the entire company. But they were abandoned by senior leadership—me, the entrepreneur and the one in charge. This was a huge lesson in accountability and my attendance to my business.

By August, I became so severely depressed that even getting out of bed was a challenge. I carried a lot of resentment with me. I hated my manager. I hated my staff. I hated myself. And I knew I couldn't quit because the bank would call the notes and I would lose everything. The burden was enormous, and I felt an overwhelming feeling of hopelessness. My Itty Bitty Shitty Committee was meeting on a daily basis.

So there I was, cloaked in a mixture of real financial distress and enormous self-doubt: "You suck, you are not good enough." The crippling depression was so bad I couldn't go into my office many days. And that broken man somehow had to make the decision whether or not to continue with the business.

I was filled with self-hatred and shame. The problem seemed too complex for me. I couldn't see a path out. I was suffering from what I later learned was called Imposter Syndrome, big-time, and I had been too ashamed to ask for help from anyone other than Greg, my older brother.

Nearly fifteen years later, my life is much better. No big surprise, as it couldn't have gotten much worse. But those years were the definition of suck. The good days were barely good enough to keep us afloat. But the truth was, I ended up $600,000 in debt in a matter of eight years. What surprises me is the way I got to the other side. As I'm writing this book, COVID-19 has shut down most of the world, and we're all reeling from watching hundreds of thousands of people die in the United States and even more worldwide. Businesses are filing for bankruptcy every day, and millions of people have been furloughed or laid off. It has been devastating.

But I know we can pivot. We've experienced economic disaster before. In the United States, we go through a recession about every ten years, almost like clockwork. The lessons I share with you in this book are the exact lessons I used to take Diversified Industrial Staffing from $600,000 in debt to being named by *Inc. 5000* as one of the fastest growing companies in the United States—an incredible six times—all in the midst and aftermath of the Great Recession of the late 2000s. This book tells the story of how to avoid the suck and achieve success by making simple but sometimes difficult decisions to strengthen your company and yourself. And it shares stories from other top leaders whom I've helped do the same. I made a big mess from 1997 through 2006, there's no denying that. But I've since turned my mess into my message so I can help others avoid or come back from their own version of suck. I know you can, too.

My Approach

I'm not a theoretical coach. I'm an actual coach who has played the game many times, learning from both my losses and my wins. I know what it's like to almost miss payroll. I know what it's like to almost go bankrupt. I *know* what it's like to have to call my own coach and confess I haven't done what I was supposed to do and was suffering additional consequences as a result.

Importantly, I have also experienced the truth that growing a business only happens when we do the hard work and grow ourselves first.

This book walks you through the process of strengthening yourself, building a solid business foundation, and course correcting.

If you're about to start a business and can't figure out where to begin, this book is for you.

If you're scaling a business and feel suffocated as you contemplate the next steps, this book is for you.

If you're pivoting a business and don't know which way to turn, this book is for you.

If you're stuck, this book is for you.

And if you're willing to be authentic, transparent, and vulnerable, this book is for you.

Please, if there's one thing I want you to remember as you read, it's this: you are not alone. No matter how bad things might seem right now, others have been there before. Some are there now. And I'm here for you. By writing this book, I'm not intending it to be a barrier between you and me—a way to transfer knowledge to you to leave you on your own. Instead, I'm writing this book to begin a relationship with you. If you need help, accountability, or additional support, I'm here for you. Email me at Todd@ ExtraordinaryAdvisors.com. I'm here to help.

I know that by the end of this book, you will have found many friends in similar situations who are now at the top of their game. I know you can do the same, too. And while the solutions are really just a series of simple actions, it won't be easy. But I know you can do it. I've never met an entrepreneur who couldn't.

Our Path To Success

Broken into two simple parts, *From Suck to Success* is your framework for starting up, building up, or pivoting through change in the pursuit of extraordinary entrepreneurship.

In the first part, we do the internal work, helping you identify and improve your mind-set, leadership, and goal setting, or as I teach it, intention setting. First, in Chapter 1, we'll figure out our mind-sets—what's holding us back or keeping us stuck. I'll share how discovering your "why," or *ikigai*, is so pivotal to finding success in both business and your personal life. In Chapter 2, I'll walk you through the ATV leadership-improvement process. It's a concept I've developed throughout my years of coaching to help entrepreneurs become Authentic, Transparent, and Vulnerable (ATV) in a productive way. ATV is one of the most critical steps in moving us forward in conscious leadership and avoiding a world of suck. In Chapter 3, I'll help you set intentions, rather than expectations, in your business and share why that subtle difference is so important. Finally, in Chapter 4, I'll share a simple four-step process you can use to guide you as you move forward in becoming the best entrepreneur you can be. The four-step process can help you identify and adjust whenever your mind-set, leadership, or intention setting is veering in the wrong direction.

In the second part of the book, we do the external work to improve your business operations. We start with Chapter 5, in which we discuss the looping line of success. Chapter 5 helps you set up your business to perform differently in the future than it has to date, starting with building a strong culture within your organization. Next, we will move onto Chapter 6, empowering yourself through team members. Success is all about investing in employees, fostering healthy organizations, and creating extraordinary cultures for our businesses to thrive. I'll also share simple but powerful strategies to do exactly that.

In Chapters 7 and 8, we go deep into tactical strategies to achieve extraordinary success, even in the worst of times. By this point in the book, you will have everything you need to reshape your mind-set, leadership, and intention setting. You will also know how to build a strong culture that empowers your team members to perform. These two final chapters give you the tactical tools for achieving extraordinary success and building upon the foundational principles, from increasing margins to designing the life of your dreams. If you've done the work to implement the strategies from Chapters 1 through 6, Chapters 7 and 8 will help you unlock the business and life of your dreams. I refer to it as building your life by design.

Back in 2006, I never would have thought this book was possible. Now, I see the limitless possibilities that direction and discipline can give any business owner. I'll give you the direction over the rest of the book. All you need to add is the discipline. And if you want help building that muscle and making the tough decisions like I had to make, email me. I know how valuable it was to have a coach in my brother, Greg, guiding and pushing me along. I'd be happy to guide you through your turnaround, too.

Part 1:
Taking Inventory

Chapter 1

Figure Out Your Mind-Set First

"The obstacles that we think most impede us from realizing our deepest wishes can actually hasten their fulfillment."
— Gabriele Oettingen, Rethinking Positive Thinking

Without exception, the greatest factor that determines whether your business and life will suck three years from now is your mind-set today. It really is that simple. Your success as an entrepreneur almost always results from how you look at the world. All of the rest is the details you can learn along the way. But if you look at the world in a way that promotes success, you will become successful. It's only a matter of time. If not, you will end up stuck in a stressful, costly world of suck.

While the idea that your mind-set determines your future might seem ominous to you, the good news is that it's not very complicated to reprogram our brains. It's actually pretty simple to shift your mind-set. However, it's not easy. It takes a lot of hard work. But it's simple. In fact, I've never met an entrepreneur who couldn't develop a mind-set that set themselves up for success. I've met many who didn't, but I've yet to meet one who *couldn't*.

To use an analogy, if your business and your life were a car, your mind-set would be the fuel. You need the right type and amount of fuel for your car to run. The same is true with your mind-set and success. If you use the wrong fuel—in this case, the wrong mind-set—your car won't run, and your engine will become damaged. Try putting unleaded fuel in a car with a diesel engine, or vice versa, and see what I mean. (Actually, please don't try that; it really *will* damage your car.) Only the right type of fuel—in this case, the right mind-set—will allow your car to move forward. And what about the amount of fuel? If you don't continually add fuel to your car, it will eventually stop. You can't just fill it up one time and drive it for years.

You need to keep filling up your car with the right type of fuel. In our case, you need to keep filling up your business and personal life with the right perspective, the right mind-set.

When I hit bottom, as much as I thought what got me there was a collection of bad decisions, the truth was it all started with having the wrong mind-set. I was using the wrong fuel for my engine—trying to be a big staffing company, build a big team, and be everything to everyone. I also stopped filling up my engine with fuel. Had I connected regularly with other business owners or hired a coach to walk with me along the way, their influence on me would have shifted my mind-set and kept my engine topped off from 1997 until 2006. Instead, I was running on the fumes of the wrong type of thinking for almost a decade. When something went wrong, I didn't seek new or better information. I went back to doing more of what got me in the mess in the first place. A friend of mine refers to our tendency to fall back on the familiar, even if it means digging a deeper hole, as "saluting the flag of the past." That phrase really resonated with me when I heard it the first time. Sometimes, we need to let go of the flag of the past and look forward to the flag of the future.

After hiring Greg as my coach to help me, I started learning to shift my mind-set. That was powerful. The more I shifted my thinking, the more my path forward became clearer. I learned what to say yes to and, almost more importantly, what to say no to by identifying what I was unwilling to accept moving forward. Almost immediately after starting to shift my mind-set, my business and personal lives both began to improve.

In this chapter, I'll walk you through the process and benefit of shifting your mind-set that I've refined since 2006, beginning with Greg's work with me and then as I helped other entrepreneurs avoid or come back from their own version of suck. I'll do so within the context of helping you overcome the most common entrepreneurial struggles from a mind-set perspective.

The strategies I share in this chapter are meant to help you through the biggest mind-set struggles entrepreneurs face. These are the tools you need to shift your own mind-set. They will also prepare you for the next part of navigating the world of entrepreneurship: strengthening your leadership skills. The more you practice these, the better you will get at avoiding landing in your own world of suck. It will take practice. It will be hard. But it will be well worth it as you start achieving more and more success.

The Best Firefighter And Chief Arsonist

One common struggle entrepreneurs face is that they spend too much of their day putting out fires. That leaves them less time to do the most important work in their business. It also stretches them thin from a personal perspective, so they end up overworked, stressed out, and unfulfilled.
Are you spending all day putting out fires?

Do you struggle to get ahead with your workload because there's so much on your to-do list?

Have you spent years telling yourself that you need to better train team members but haven't had a break long enough to do so because you are putting out so many fires?

If you answer yes to any of these questions, congratulations. You're your company's best firefighter. This role is important because it can keep a company going for a long time. Fires come up in every business. These businesses need firefighters on the inside to prevent those fires from spreading.

So many business owners I coach complain to me that they spend all their days "putting out fires." I get it. That's how I felt for my entire first decade at Diversified Industrial Staffing, too. I spent every day putting out fire after fire, keeping the business open for nearly a decade before the flames got too big for me to control any longer. Every day, it was fire after fire. I'd swoop in and save the day and then move onto the next fire. That was my *Groundhog Day*. I'd head to the office, put out fires all day, and head home. The next day, I'd head to the office, put out more fires, and head home. I'd do that day after day until everything collapsed.

The first step to getting out of that stressful routine is to shift your mindset. Sure, you will likely remain your company's best firefighter. That's not an issue. Fires will pop up in entrepreneurship. But if you're going to be your company's best firefighter, you can't just put out fires and then move on. Firefighters do much more than that. You need to complete the work of a firefighter.

Firefighters don't just put out the flames of a burning structure and then head back to the station. They also take time to research the cause of the fire and, if there are signs of arson, work with law enforcement to prosecute the arsonists.

If we know we are our companies' best firefighters, we must shift our mind-set and complete the work to identify the cause of the fire. When Greg worked with me to continue the job at Diversified Industrial Staffing, I learned that my fires were all caused by arson. We had someone inside the company who kept starting fires. Thus, the solution was to either get rid of the arsonist or prevent them from being able to start fires in the future.

Unfortunately, I learned that the arsonist at Diversified Industrial Staffing was me. If not for me, I wouldn't have had so many fires to put out. When I realized that, everything changed. Instead of seeing myself as the hero who swept in and put out fires to keep the company going, I visualized myself starting a bunch of fires and then running around putting them out until the fires grew too big for me to handle. I loved the jolt of adrenaline solving the problems. I felt like I had accomplished something that day. It was a fool's dream.

It's not just me, either. When I work with leaders who are overwhelmed by putting out fires all day, I ask them to shift their mind-set from putting out fires to completing the job. Virtually every time, my clients realize they were their company's chief arsonists, too. Some of them identified other arsonists as well, but every single one of them realized they could quickly improve their company if they just stopped starting fires themselves.

You don't have to find yourself crumpled on the pavement (or worse) to recognize that *something* has to change in your business, either. Sure, a setback could be as large as bankruptcy, or it could be as small as a mishandled meeting. What they have in common is a gut-wrenching, hair-raising feeling of regret, fear, and self-doubt that stops us in our tracks and stunts our growth. But many times, we feel overwhelmed by putting out fires all day because we don't do the work it takes to prevent fires in the first place.

As leaders, we can be the best firefighters—while also being the chief arsonists. Think about it: the scary but joyous feeling we, as entrepreneurs, get from putting out a fire can be very visceral, like a spike of dopamine. Often, we lack self-awareness around the "rush" it gives us. So we will be subversive and act as an arsonist, which is self-sabotaging long term, in exchange for the rush of putting out the fire and being seen as the savior, the only one who can put out the fire. But we can make the complex simple by merely doing something different.

As straightforward as it might sound to identify the source of fires before moving on, you won't be able to do it if you don't shift your mind-set. But it takes awareness, discipline, and continuous practice to do so. Otherwise, the stress and relief of fighting and extinguishing fires will send us right back into our own versions of *Groundhog Day*.

Identifying What You Are Unwilling To Accept

Once you commit to sifting through the ashes of all the fires you've been putting out, you're going to start seeing your business—and yourself—in a different light. The mind-set with which you examine the ashes and react to what you find will be critical to whether you continue to head toward success or fall back into a world of suck. It's so easy to see all the mistakes you and others have been making and become frustrated. And it's easy for you to let that frustration lead you to fall back into your old ways.

One of the first questions my coaching clients ask me is what they need to do to clean up their messes. After all, they're high performers used to running from fire to fire. While that's a natural question to ask, the more effective question to ask is what do they need to *stop doing* in order to achieve success. That's because the entrepreneurs also frequently struggle with being spread too thin.

Thus, when clients ask me what they need to do, I shift the question and ask them to first identify what they need to *stop doing*—what they're unwilling to accept moving forward. This is the best way to shake up stagnation and prevent the frustration you feel from sending you backward. That's why one of the first things that I do with my coaching clients is have them make a "stop-doing list." While the content of the list varies from client to client, every client I've challenged to do this has benefited greatly from the exercise.

For example, one of my coaching clients, Tom Schwab, runs a company called Interview Valet, which helps authors, speakers, and others talk directly to ideal customers through podcast interview marketing. Tom came to me already having achieved great levels of success in his business. He was making money and helping a lot of people. But he spent all day putting out fires. He was a bottleneck in his business.

I worked with Tom to sift through the ashes of several fires he had put out in his business. Like most of us, Tom realized he was spread too thin by performing administrative tasks he had no business doing. All those duties prevented him from leading his team as well as he could and giving them the systems and tools to operate independently. When Tom and I put together his stop-doing list, it quickly filled up with administrative tasks, such as entering payroll. He would spend three or four hours entering payroll every Sunday.

When I put together my stop-doing list as I was rebuilding my business, I listed being unwilling to accept that I was a victim of my employees. I used to think that my business success was limited to the employees I had on staff. While I was internalizing it as a permanent situation, Greg helped me view that thinking as temporary. He helped me see that I had the ultimate choice on who would stay and go. It took looking at my company with fresh eyes to see this, but once I did, it changed my life.

I want you to look at your company with completely fresh eyes as you do this, too. I don't care if you've been doing something for decades. If it's not the best approach for the future, write it down on the list of items you are unwilling to accept moving forward. Remind yourself that the phrase "We've always done business this way" is the sure kiss of death for long-term success. Instead, ask yourself whether you would accept that approach if you were starting your business over, or advising another business owner about best practices. Additionally, ask yourself, would you hire that employee again?

Identifying things we're not willing to accept can become stressful. Drawing a line in the sand over things that have defined our roles or businesses for years feels like a big deal. I know it did for Tom when he committed to stop doing payroll. It did for me when I committed to stop seeing myself as a victim of my employees, too. That's what makes the next part of the process so important.

The next step with your stop-doing list isn't to take the list and immediately stop doing everything on it. Instead, the next step is to put a plan in place to stop doing them as fast as reasonably possible. For example, one thing on my stop-doing list was mowing the lawn. That was easy to stop doing quickly. I could hire a kid to mow my lawn for $25 within days. However, it took Tom Schwab two years to plan and execute a successful payroll handoff for Interview Valet.

The way you see the world when it comes to the items on your list will go a long way toward determining whether you successfully outsource or delegate the items on your stop-doing list. Unfortunately, entrepreneurs often look at the tasks they perform with a fixed mind-set instead of a growth mind-set. They think they're the only one who can adequately perform the tasks. They think their way is the only or best way to perform a task. They think if something goes wrong, it will spiral downward to a world of suck. They'll lose a customer. That customer will post about it online. Eventually, the business will collapse.

Not only is a fixed mind-set incredibly stressful for the entrepreneur but it's also based on lies. For example, there's no way Tom Schwab was the only person qualified to do payroll for Interview Valet. How did I know at the time? Because millions of companies around the world did payroll without Tom's help. If he were the only person able to do payroll, no other company would be able to successfully process payroll. The same was true with Diversified Industrial Staffing. Once I allowed myself to stop looking at my team members as the only group of people who could help me, I started making tough but important decisions to find better fits for my company and train them well. (And, yes, I realize how ironic it is for the leader of a staffing company to be stuck in a fixed mind-set about staffing. But that's how strong a fixed mind-set can be. It can block out all logical thinking, and it did for me.)

We must shift away from seeing our world through a fixed mind-set and move to looking at it with a growth mind-set. *Of course* someone else could do payroll for Interview Valet. *Of course* others could help me run

Diversified Industrial Staffing. We must go into our stop-doing list with the mind-set that we have options. Others can do everything we can. Many times, they can do it better and cheaper than we can. And working our way through our stop-doing list with that mind-set opens up incredible opportunities.

Chief arsonists and firefighters love having things to accomplish, to cross off. They're used to having a lot to do. They're used to being busy. That's what makes the stop-doing list so powerful. It gives these leaders a sometimes-long list of tasks to hand off. Even better, the more they work their way through the list, they more they find that the things they had been doing that they thought were essential to the business could really be handed off or outsourced. Many times, they find others to do the task even better than they did.

The more they hand off or outsource, the more they can shift to driving revenue or just enjoying their life outside of work. In other words, they shift to doing the things they really *should* be doing as CEOs and the things they really want to be doing as people outside of work.

Creating Your First Stop-Doing List

It's time. Make your first stop-doing list today. I don't care if it's Saturday night and you finally caught a break from your firefighting. You don't need to be in the midst of sifting through the ashes to start listing things. You know at least a few things that you need to stop doing, so why wait? Why not start now?

Keep it simple. Take a shot at creating your first stop-doing list and keep it handy so you can add to it as you continue to put out fires. The first thing I added to my stop-doing list was mowing my lawn. It didn't take much for me to add it. Someone had challenged me about how much I valued my time shortly before I made my list. I had been thinking about it for a while and came up with the figure of $500 per hour. So when I sat down to create my first stop-doing list, I started listing tasks I could outsource for cheaper than $500 per hour. Mowing my lawn was the first thing to come to mind. It took me two hours to mow my lawn. That meant I was spending $1,000 of time mowing my lawn when I could have gotten some kid to do it for $25.

With entrepreneurs, it's important to know this is a holistic exercise and includes adding business and personal tasks to our lists. Look at everything you're doing inside and outside of your business as you create your list. This is critical because we have a tendency to try to separate our business from our personal lives. I believe it's because we've been trained to search for the illusive work-life balance. So our natural reaction is to look at work and life differently. But the truth is, there's no such thing as work-life balance for entrepreneurs. Entrepreneurs play in the game of work-life integration. Therefore, stop forcing yourself to look at the twenty-four hours you have each day in terms of business hours and life hours. Instead, take those twenty-four hours and fill them with activities that help your business and personal life.

With a stop-doing list that includes business and life tasks, start to see your world differently and free up time to start doing things that are important to both your business and personal life. If you want to spend more time investing in your personal relationship, start doing date nights twice a month. Free up time to do so. Make those an appointment on your calendar and honor that commitment.

This is important. Entrepreneurs have a tendency to only add business activities to the time they free up with their stop-doing list. Be sure to add things that lift you up on a personal level, too. You'll find yourself much more fulfilled and effective in your business if you do.

Here are some questions to ask yourself as you prepare your first stop-doing list:
- What does a successful next ten years look like in my business?
- What do I want my legacy to be within this organization?
- What behaviors as a leader do I need to change or initiate in others to see this change occur?
- What do I want my personal life to look like?

Keep these questions top-of-mind as you explore what to add to your stop-doing list. If something is inconsistent with your answers to these questions, consider adding it to your stop-doing list.

Uncertainty vs. Change

After creating your first stop-doing list, you're likely to be in a much healthier mind-set than before. It might seem like you have a lot to do, but you will have a list of tasks to start outsourcing, delegating, or even eliminating. Start offloading or eliminating the simple things right away and create a plan for the other items to keep that momentum going.

While your mind-set will be healthier, it's important to keep a growth mind-set going forward because many entrepreneurs struggle with so much uncertainty and change. It sounds strange, but many people are more comfortable with a miserable situation they're used to than an uncertain path toward a better future that they're not used to. That discomfort could lead them to fall back into their old fixed-minded ways if they're not careful.

To keep our growth mind-set moving forward, we must recognize that, as leaders, what we may consider personal and private attitudes and actions are a direct pipeline to the performance of our businesses. It's understandable that we want as much certainty as possible. Desiring certainty is really a craving for prediction—trying to figure out what's going to happen or what to expect. We want to be safe. Unfortunately, that mentality is a falsehood that doesn't exist. When we choose the pursuit of certainty over the reality of uncertainty, we stop achieving. In order to change our businesses or grow our skills as leaders, we need to embrace uncertainty.

Change occurs when we are unwilling to accept our current reality, and for many of us, the escape route from being the Best Firefighter and the Chief Arsonist begins with one step:

- Are you unwilling to accept the current state of your business? Hire a coach.
- Are you unwilling to accept your current weight? Eat differently. Join a gym.
- Are you unwilling to accept an underperforming or toxic employee? Get them to leave your company or terminate them.
- Are you unwilling to accept your miserable job? Network. Post your résumé online.

You can decide in simply one day what you are unwilling to accept and make the changes from there. Engage with what isn't working.

Entrepreneurial coach Dan Sullivan writes about what
ceiling of complexity."[4] It's the point in each and every stag
which people can't grow any further using their existing se __
knowledge. "As you progress in your growth, you gain experience by
solving problems and transacting business," Sullivan writes. "However, this
experience often comes at a price: complexity. Each problem you solve,
each transaction you make, and each hurdle you overcome adds to this
complexity to the point where it holds you back from future growth of
capability, performance, and achievement. You become overwhelmed by
the messes, 'stuff,' complications, conflicts, and contradictions that come
from doing things a certain way for a long time."[5]

Stagnation causes more stagnation. But mastering your mind-set can start
by asking yourself two simple questions:
- What is my pain?
- Have I reached a "ceiling of complexity"?

Remember, we can't tackle a problem until we realize there is a problem. So
falling into some common leadership traps stemming from the mind-sets I
mentioned earlier—obsessing over cash flow, feeling like an outsider—can
prevent us from recovering, listening, and focusing on what matters.

Suck vs. Success
Examples of a stuck mind-set include feeling like:
- "I am the business; the business is me."
- "I'm a rugged individualist, but now I need to ask others for help."
- "We've always done business this way."

And a prime example of a mind-set ready for change is when we
say to ourselves:
- "Old behaviors that once served me well no longer work."
- "I am not the only person in the world who can perform this task."

Solving Problems By Practicing Creative—Not Reactive—Thinking
How much of your time do you spend reacting to other people or the
circumstances of the day? If you're stuck extinguishing fires, you likely

spend more time than you'd prefer in reactive mode. Likewise, if you're constantly feeling the need to do everything yourself to get it done, you're probably spending more time than you'd prefer in reactive mode.

And what do you do when something doesn't go according to plan? Do you feel your blood pressure rise? Do you feel the intensity of the situation go up? If so, you're like most entrepreneurs.

How you respond in those moments is what determines whether your day will suck or end successfully. If you practice reactive thinking, your day will suck. If you practice creative thinking, it will end in success almost every single time.

Here's an example of how this works. Let's say you run a content marketing business. Someone calls you up and wants a discount. When this happens, many entrepreneurs fear that they'll lose the sale if they don't offer a discount. They have other clients who pay full price, but maybe times are tough, and a new project could really help out.

How would you respond in this situation? One of the most impactful lessons my coach, Dr. Daniel Friedland, taught me was the difference between practicing reactive thinking and practicing creative thinking.

When we practice reactive thinking, we might roll up our sleeves and try to solve this discount problem on our own. If we fear we'll lose the client, we might simply agree to the discount. Or we might get angry, feel disrespected, and steer the conversation somewhere unproductive.

On the other hand, if we practice a creative mind-set, we'll try to find a solution that defends our pricing model in a way that makes both our new client and us happy. I'll continue using this example to explain my Extraordinary Four (E-4) Process to shift from reactive thinking to creative thinking at the end of this chapter.

For now, I want to share what Dr. Friedland taught me about the creative and reactive mind-sets so you can begin to recognize moments when you fall into reactive thinking. The reactive mind-set, explains Dr. Friedland in his book *Leading Well from Within: A Neuroscience and Mindfulness-Based Framework for Conscious Leadership,* is

> where we feel threatened with fear, stress, self-doubt, ego, and conflict; where an unconscious and reflexive series of protective responses can dominate our psyche and ripple through our actions, activating similar experiences in others that can instantly drain energy and fragment teams as well as families.[6]

The creative mind-set, meanwhile, is one

> where with conscious awareness, self-compassion, and courage, we can lean in and grow, even in our most challenging circumstances. Inspiration, energy, and empathy are present, and innovation can flourish, enabling a team to work well together with transparency and trust and become aligned in a shared vision to more fully focus its collective energy to serve others and something larger than themselves.[7]

Let's return to my curb-crying moment. Clearly, I was in a reactive mind-set, full of fear and stress as I contemplated the end of my business. Thanks to intentionally focusing on five positive things, however, I was able to shift into a creative mind-set. Sure, it took a while for me to lean in and grow, but it happened.

As Dr. Friedland writes, "[l]eaders, and their ability to be aware of and navigate stress, uncertainty, and self-doubt in any given situation can profoundly influence which mind-set dominates."[8]

Some of the top tips I've learned from Dr. Friedland about shifting mind-set from reactive to creative include:

- Focus on satisfaction, not happiness. You earn satisfaction from taking your own hero's journey, at times. It's a reflection upon the highs and lows of the journey that results in a satisfying outcome. Happiness is a spike of dopamine. It's not sustainable and is short-lived.
- Listen to absorb, not respond.
- It all starts with you. In order to fix your business, your relationships, your parenting, or your coaching, you must work on yourself first.
- Practice appreciative inquiry.
- Approach all issues and conflicts with massive curiosity.[9]

Setting Intentions, Taking Action, And Iterating Forward

Another common struggle entrepreneurs face is when we find ourselves up against unfilled expectations. If the content marketing entrepreneur goes into sales calls with a rigid structure and expects every client to choose between two or three options, she would be setting herself up for disappointment. If we plan our business down to the smallest detail and expect everything to work out as planned, we'd be setting ourselves up for the same disappointment. And although most entrepreneurs would tell you never to expect everything to go according to plan, many run their businesses as if everything was going to work out exactly according to plan.

They don't intend to, but they do. So when things go wrong, they spiral into a world of suck. That's because we can only control the next step we take. After the first step, something else is going to happen. Someone is going to react to what we do. Something is going to change. So why plan your business based on the expectation that thirteen things will happen in a row in order to achieve an expected outcome?

Expectations are dangerous. They're poisonous to our mind-set and our businesses. Instead of setting expectations, I want you to set intentions, take action, and iterate as you go. Set your intended result. Plan your first step. Take action. Then plan the next step based on what happens after the first step so you are still heading toward your intended result. While that sounds tedious, as entrepreneurs we can make decisions quickly—especially if we're in the right frame of mind.

For example, my intention was to somehow pay off $600,000 in debt, but I didn't know how. So I created a strategy and took action. It was in the midst of the Great Recession, and I had to find companies that would still hire people. Yeah, that was pretty hard to do. I didn't know companies who were hiring. I didn't have relationships with many companies. And, as you know, I don't like cold calling—at all.

But I had a list of companies I had worked with before, and my plan was to start calling as many people as I could to learn how I could place people at their company. That was as far as I had planned: I intended to pay off debt, and I planned to call as many people as possible to figure out how to place people.

As I started calling people, my fears were confirmed. Nobody was eager to hire. So, I iterated. Before I got off the phone with people, I'd ask two questions: "If you could only hire one person when you come out of the recession, what role would that be? And what skill set do you expect to be looking for when you come out of the recession?" Every time, they would pause and answer something like, "If I could just find a CNC machinist who could program in Mazak-Mazatrol, I'd be interested." (That's technical language for someone who can program software to automate complex machining tools and 3-D printers. Mazak-Mazatrol is basically Microsoft Office for complex machines.)

I kept asking that question over and over again. That was my strategy to understand what companies were looking for from a staffing perspective. If I could find those Mazak-Mazatrol people, I could place them easier than if I tried to continue what I had been doing up to that point. That would help me achieve my intention much better than to try to place people that companies didn't need. I couldn't expect what I had done before to work. But I could take action and adjust to what the market was telling me.

Confronting Your Brutal Reality

Remember when you were a kid and you just knew your parents were about to deliver some bad news? Maybe you were moving out of your awesome home in Arizona to somewhere new in New England. Maybe Chuck E. Cheese was already booked the day of your planned birthday party. Maybe you ran out of Fruity Pebbles. It doesn't matter. As a kid, you likely went straight into the reactive mind-set—often taking the form of a temper tantrum. (We still do this as adults, just in slightly more subtle ways, such as pouring another drink, blasting AC/DC through our AirPods, or bingeing on Netflix.)

In *Good to Great*, Jim Collins calls upon leaders to "confront the brutal facts" when faced with a crappy situation if they want to pull out of it.[10] As an example, he raises the contrast between supermarket chains A&P and Kroger. Both in the same industry with similar challenges, A&P suffered tremendous failure while Kroger did not. Why? As Collins explains, "[o]ne of these two companies confronted the brutal facts of reality head-on and completely changed its entire system in response; the other stuck its head in the sand."[11]

In other words, A&P demonstrated a reactive mind-set response to a failing system. It continued moving forward with the same system and expected everything to work out. And it didn't work out, causing A&P to file for bankruptcy two times before shuttering its business. Kroger kicked in a creative mind-set, setting an intention to recreate itself using a new model and adjust along the way. Today, Kroger is valued at more than $25 billion.

The trajectory took years and years to see itself through. It took tremendous patience and discipline for Kroger's leadership to see it through to the multi-billion-dollar powerhouse it is today. It had to confront the brutal facts that what it and A&P were doing hadn't been working and then set intentions, take action, and adjust.

So how do we learn from A&P and Kroger? We have to do the same. We have to maintain a creative mind-set while suffering through the brutal facts about our businesses. That can lead to strong feelings of remorse, stress, and fear that can drain not only our energy but that of our employees and even families. With me, I needed to confront the brutal facts that my entire business model needed to change. I couldn't compete against the big staffing agencies and survive. Margins were too low. The economy was too weak. And I had too much debt to pay down. I also had to confront the brutal fact that I needed to replace my team with people who were better fits moving forward. Only after I confronted that reality could I muster the confidence to try something different.

The Stockdale Paradox
"You must never confuse faith that you will prevail in the end—which you can never afford to lose—with the discipline to confront the most brutal facts of your current reality, whatever they might be."—Vice Admiral James Stockdale

Retain faith that you will prevail in the end, regardless of the difficulties.

and at the same time

Confront the most brutal facts of your current reality, whatever they might be.

Another way to look at our brutal reality is through what author Jim Collins termed the Stockdale Paradox. For those unfamiliar with this framework, the Stockdale Paradox tells us that we must retain faith that we will prevail in the end while simultaneously confronting the most brutal facts of our current reality. It comes from Navy Vice Admiral James Stockdale, who was imprisoned for nearly eight years in Vietnam during the Vietnam War. Stockdale was tortured more than fifteen times during that period and frequently battled with his captors in an effort to save his fellow prisoners. His efforts earned him a Congressional Medal of Honor, and he was one of the most highly decorated officers in the history of the Navy.

Collins met with Stockdale to discuss his ordeal. During the meeting, Stockdale said he never doubted that not only would he get out but he would also prevail in the end and turn the experience into the defining event of his life, which, in retrospect, he said he would not trade for anything in the world.

While not a trained psychologist, Stockdale practiced and shared a psychological duality Collins coined the Stockdale Paradox. "In wrestling with life's challenges," writes Collins, "the Stockdale Paradox has proved powerful for coming back from difficulties not weakened but stronger— not just for me but for all those who've learned the lesson and tried to apply it."

The Stockdale Paradox rings true years later. As I'm writing this book, we are in the midst of coping with the coronavirus pandemic. Before COVID-19 hit, my old model of growing my coaching business involved building awareness and generating business by speaking from stages around the world. In March 2020, however, all events began shutting down.

I had two choices: double down on what worked in the past and ignore the brutal reality of my circumstances or confront the brutal reality and adjust. I chose to confront the brutal reality and adjust in a few different ways:

1.   I used the added time I had available to write this book. I had begun the book before the pandemic hit, but the shutdown opened up more time for me, at least at first.
2.   I started speaking on webinars and other virtual stages.
3.   I began looking at using different ways to get my message out in

front of my ideal customers. Beyond webinars, I have used Facebook and other social media platforms to serve people.

4. I created different pricing and delivery models because I no longer had to travel two days to conduct training for one day. Instead of sitting with a leadership team for six hours in Fort Lauderdale, Florida, for example, I can do a four-hour Zoom call with the leadership team, with a tighter agenda, because I know that people can't sit still forever on a Zoom call.

5. I started inviting business owners to a phone call to help them as they struggle through their own brutal realities. I knew they needed help. And because I had more time available, I decided I would offer free coaching just to help as many people as possible, with no ulterior motives.

I did this all while retaining faith that I'll prevail in the end, regardless of the difficulties—and all while confronting the brutal facts of my current reality. In the end, I know my business is going to be stronger two years from now than it was two years ago. I will have many more avenues to speak and many more ways to find coaching clients. In fact, all of those efforts started paying dividends even during the pandemic.

What Do You Really Want?

"That's the hardest question I've found for many people to answer. I had to answer that for myself because what I thought I wanted, what I thought would fill the emptiness of that five-year-old who had lost everybody important to him, was 'things'— money, toys, houses, whatever. What I really found, what I really get to do with my clients, is helping them define success related to something that matters to them. And more often than not, it does not have to do with material items. For me, success is doing what I want, when I want, with whom I want to do it, as often as possible."—from my "Discover Your Talent" podcast.

Rethinking Positive Thinking

Let me confront a common struggle many leaders have as they work on their mind-set. Many leaders—and even coaches—emphasize the value of having a positive mind-set, even while confronting the brutal reality of their current situation. While I do support maintaining a positive mind-set, I do so with one big point of caution: a positive mind-set alone won't improve your situation if it's not accompanied with action. That's why we shift from reactive thinking to creative thinking by setting intention and then taking action. We don't just set an intention to improve and wait.

However, research tells us that mind-set is more complicated than just flipping a switch from negative to positive. For example, in the book *Rethinking Positive Thinking: Inside the New Science of Motivation,* author and psychologist Gabriele Oettingen shares the results of more than twenty years of research in the field of human motivation to reveal why the conventional wisdom about positive thinking doesn't work. She shares how people actually make changes and overcome the obstacles that get in their way when pursuing meaningful change. (I highly recommend reading *Rethinking Positive Thinking.* It's a well-written book that dives deep into one of the biggest challenges business leaders face when it comes to mind-set.)

Oettingen, like Stockdale, rebuffs naked optimism. Among other examples, she points to politics, analyzing presidential speeches from 1993 to 2009. "In particular," she writes, "we tested to see whether positive thinking in the speeches correlated with 'long-term indicators of economic performance.'" Oettingen and her team found a "clear relationship: the more positive the inaugural address for a given presidential term, the lower the GDP and the higher the unemployment rates were in the following presidential term."

Dreaming is just that: dreaming. And when we simply engage in naked positive thinking, it can actually make things worse, Oettingen explains. Specifically, Oettingen found that when people truly believe their goals will come true, they could fall into the trap of inaction. Their positive thinking lulls them to not take action because they believe everything will work out in the end. For example, Oettingen looked at university graduates to study the effect of positive thinking in job searches. What she found was that students who thought positively about their job prospects earned less money and received fewer job offers over the following two years than those who were less optimistic. Why? Because the ones who weren't worried sent out fewer applications.

So what do you do about it? First, you need to be aware of these tendencies. If you're a positive thinker, your brain quite literally lulls you into inaction. Second, you need to do something about it. The simple four-part test I share with you in Chapter 4 will help you with that. For now, what's most important is being aware of the tendency to lull ourselves into inaction.

Diagnosing Your Mind-Set

Author Zig Ziglar famously said people need to do a "daily checkup from the neck up" to make sure they move forward with the right mind-set. In this chapter, I've shared tools, exercises, and resources for you to identify and shift your mind-set to keep you from a world of suck and instead head toward one of tremendous success.

As you move forward, I want you to continue to develop the ability to self-diagnose whether your mind-set is in a healthy space. The tools I shared will help you do that. In addition, I want you to keep in mind that the very characteristics creating a ladder to success are also those that can tumble us to the ground. Consider this report from *Entrepreneur* magazine, which highlights twelve signs of an entrepreneurial mind-set:

1. You take action.
2. You're scared.
3. You're resourceful.
4. You obsess over cash flow.
5. You don't ask for permission.
6. You're fearless.
7. You welcome change.
8. You love a challenge.
9. You consider yourself an outsider.
10. You recover quickly.
11. You listen.
12. You focus on what matters (when you figure out what matters).[12]

Do these sound familiar? Many such mind-set signs could go either way in leadership. Taking action could mean securing the next great deal or making a $1-million mistake. Obsessing over cash flow could represent financial savviness, or it could be a sign that your business is stuck. Fearlessness and feeling like an outsider can easily turn into fearfulness and feeling incredibly lonely in the leadership journey.

Use these tools to get and keep your mind-set in a healthy place. Be the entrepreneur who is willing to do the hard work to build a better, more fulfilling, and less stressful business. And if you find yourself struggling with mind-set, you'll want to keep my simple Four-Step Process discussed in Chapter 4 close by.

Ask For Help

Before we move onto Chapter 2, I want to encourage you. Mind-set is tough. It's the biggest thing that separates suck from success. And one of the best ways to maintain a healthy mind-set is to not be afraid to ask for help. From a coach to a group of colleagues to trusted friends, you have many options for getting help.

I learned this lesson the hard way. My mind-set since I can remember has been that I could always only rely upon myself: "I can always take care of myself. I don't need other people."

When I was five, my father died unexpectedly; he was only forty-five. My older brother was a senior in high school, and he left the state to take advantage of an athletic scholarship. My older sister was getting married and moved to Arizona with her new husband. And my mom, who was my primary caregiver and the prototypical stay-at-home mom of the 1970s, had to go to work.

So, within ninety days, all the people in my life left me as a five-year-old. The story I told myself after that was, "I can't rely on other people. They can disappear fast. I can only rely upon myself." That's a great trait for an entrepreneur—until it's not.

I carried that mind-set with me when I started my business. I'm going to rely on me, I said. I learned all the parts of the job. I learned accounting, I learned operations, and I told myself I could do it all. In growing and scaling the company, I was hiring people. But I was not really empowering those people. And I was not leading those people correctly, yet. So I got $600,000 into debt.

After hitting rock bottom, I gave up and got help, first from Greg, and then from a whole bunch of others. I read. I hired a coach to help me get out of debt. And I learned to identify the mind-set I'd had. I forced myself to get rid of that mind-set of "I can do everything; I can be all things to all people."

My entire life changed when I finally asked for help. Today, my motto when I find myself stuck is *I need to get help.*

Please learn from my mistakes and practice getting help from the start.

Insights

- All change starts from within.
- You are not alone. We all have fears and self-doubts.
- No one has all the answers. Ask for help when you've reached the ceiling of complexity.

Questions For Reflection

- What's the No. 1 negative belief you're holding onto that's holding you back?
- Who can you reach out to in your network for help when you've reached the ceiling of complexity?
- Do you start fires in your life just so you can put them out? Whether it's business, family, or other relationships, what are you doing that's counterproductive to what you want?

Action Steps

- Say to yourself, "Next time I enter into my reactive mind-set, I will pivot into a creative mind-set."
- Pick one person in your life that you will proactively listen to in practice—listening to absorb, not to respond.
- Write out your own version of an example from your life that would mirror a Stockdale Paradox.

Additional Resources

Friedland, Daniel. *Leading Well from Within: A Neuroscience and Mindfulness-Based Framework for Conscious Leadership.* San Diego: SuperSmartHealth, 2016.

Oettingen, Gabriele. *Rethinking Positive Thinking: Inside the New Science of Motivation.* New York: Current, 2015.

Also visit ExtraordinaryAdvisors.com for more exclusive coaching tips.

Chapter 2

Learning To Be Authentic, Transparent, And Vulnerable

"It is not the critic who counts; not the man who points out how the strong man stumbles, or where the doer of deeds could have done them better. The credit belongs to the man who is actually in the arena, whose face is marred by dust and sweat and blood; who strives valiantly; who errs, who comes short again and again, because there is no effort without error and shortcoming; but who does actually strive to do the deeds; who knows great enthusiasms, the great devotions; who spends himself in a worthy cause; who at the best knows in the end the triumph of high achievement, and who at the worst, if he fails, at least fails while daring greatly, so that his place shall never be with those cold and timid souls who neither know victory nor defeat."—Teddy Roosevelt

Lumpy couches. Old tires. Collections of David Hasselhoff memorabilia. These are just some of the countless items that the bright blue trucks of 1-800-GOT-JUNK? picks up every day at more than 200 locations across three countries. As they say, one man's trash is another man's treasure, and perhaps it's no truer than in the case of the 1-800-GOT JUNK? empire that Brian Scudamore built.

I know Brian through the Gathering of Titans entrepreneurial program that I'm a member of at MIT in Boston. He impressed me with how well he runs his company—and how much he loves his work. But what impressed me even more was Brian's approach to leadership and resiliency. Specifically, the only diploma Brian received was from kindergarten. He never finished high school. He never finished college. With his background, the last position you'd expect to see on his résumé would be the founder and CEO of a company that generates hundreds of millions of dollars a year in revenue.

So how did Brian lift himself up from what most people would categorize as a failed education? He talked all about the keys to his success in his brilliantly titled book *WTF?! (Willing to Fail): How Failure Can Be Your*

Key to Success. As Brian explains, "[f]ailure is a temporary condition. Afterward, it is a lesson learned. It is wisdom gained." [13]

It's great advice, and so true. But we're not talking about a simple life lesson here. We're talking about a guy without a high school diploma running a conglomerate. That's far from the equivalent of learning a lesson that moves you forward. I asked Brian to sit down with me and talk a little deeper about this. "Those failures just taught me that I didn't learn in the traditional sense," he tells me today. "You think that I have not met an entrepreneur or someone who's been a successful leader of the world who hasn't failed over and over and over again? You can take the Michael Jordans of the world and his story of not making the high school basketball team, but learning from those failures made him more determined and more focused on what mattered and propelled him forward. My philosophy is, 'Failure is a central ingredient.'"

Brian failed to graduate from high school but didn't let that define him. Instead, he let it drive him forward. In his case, Brian looked beyond all the complex lessons he could have learned from his failures—like whether the educational system played a role in his lack of a diploma. Instead, he taught himself to view it in much simpler terms—he didn't learn the same way other kids did. That was all his lack of education told him. It wouldn't define him. It wouldn't preclude him from being a CEO of a big company. It just meant he lacked a diploma.

Brian also knew that leadership came from being himself, being honest, and being willing to take risks. Brain is perhaps the best example of how to achieve success through a model I call ATV—Authentic, Transparent, and Vulnerable—leadership. When Brian was five years into his business, for example, he had to fire eleven people (basically his entire company). He describes it as "an awfully dark, painful time in my life." So how did he lead through such a challenging time? "I took ownership and accountability. People could see that I had made a mistake," he says. "I was authentic, I was transparent, and I was vulnerable. And it paid off in the end, because I've built a half-billion dollar business by finding the right people and treating them right."

In this chapter, we'll discuss the ATV model and how it can apply to you, your teams, and your companies because of the level of trust it builds. After you build yourself up as a leader through ATV, I'm confident you will agree that it's the only way to get good—with yourself, with your leadership teams, and with your clients or customers. You'll also likely agree that the only way to have restful nights and to make good, clear decisions is by being authentic, transparent, and vulnerable.

But there are also struggles that come along with the ATV model. For example, when we open ourselves up to concede that we're imperfect leaders, we often bump up against something called "Imposter Syndrome," which I'll discuss. In the end, the struggles we face because of ATV are much better for you and your business than the struggles you will face if you *don't* lead through authenticity, transparency, and vulnerability.

Specifically, pushing through challenges that arise from ATV make you a stronger, better leader. Challenges that arise from not leading through authenticity, transparency, and vulnerability lead to inefficiencies, poor team performance, and, eventually, disaster.

Finding Strength By Combining Vulnerability And Objectivity

When I introduce the idea of leading through vulnerability to leaders, it's hardly ever met with excitement. Leaders aren't used to being vulnerable, and the thought of it is naturally uncomfortable. I encourage them, though. We can't motivate teams to perform through false bravado. It might push people in the short term, but in the long term, people will do just enough work to not get fired and the best ones will rush to greener pastures.

I also don't encourage leaders to flip a switch and show up the following morning talking about how their parents didn't hug them enough. That's not ATV leadership. Instead, we must continue to work on and improve how we look at our business and ourselves. We must be willing to admit when we don't know something, concede that others can do things better than us, and be willing to apologize when we do something wrong. It's like exercising a muscle. When we first start working out, we don't slap the heaviest weights on the bar and try to bench press it with nobody spotting us. We'd likely crush our skulls, if we could even lift the bar off the bench. We start with lighter weights and ask someone to spot us.

Two of the best ways that I've continued to learn and exercise my ATV muscles is through mentorship and continuous learning. This ensures I grow my knowledge and have accountability to do the hard work that it takes to grow my business and support my team members and clients. I get mentorship and accountability by hiring coaches, like Greg, as well as by joining groups of other entrepreneurs, such as Entrepreneurs' Organization (EO), to surround myself with people who have similar goals as I do. I get information by reading books, taking courses, and listening to podcasts. EO and other groups I've joined also give me access to top-quality information to help me continue to grow.

If you're just getting started building your mind-set muscle, two of my favorite books to read are *Dare to Lead,* by Brené Brown, and *Good to Great,* by Jim Collins.

In *Dare to Lead,* Brown provides deep answers to one of the greatest mind-set challenges entrepreneurs face: being vulnerable. Simply put, vulnerability is recognizing what you don't do well and then raising your hand and asking for help. In your workplace, it might look like apologizing to an employee who you just treated poorly. In your path to growing as a leader, it might look like hiring a coach or joining an accountability group.

Many entrepreneurs won't be vulnerable because they see vulnerability as a sign of weakness. However, entrepreneurs who do not allow themselves to be vulnerable in a healthy way become even more exhausted. They only work on being exhausted in a healthy way when they've hit rock bottom or recognize that what they have been doing is no longer working for them. Brown will teach you healthy ways to be vulnerable in *Dare to Lead.*

In *Good to Great,* Collins teaches lessons from some of the biggest and most resilient companies in the world.[15] In doing so, he shares objective lessons we can use to evaluate whether we are lying to others or ourselves about the health of our businesses. *Good to Great* is my favorite business book of all time by leaps and bounds because it takes a very analytical, data-driven approach to looking at success. It takes a very clear look at greatness in many different facets, across many different industries, and in many different ways. When it was written, many of the concepts Collins teaches were novel. Today, they're standard fare in entrepreneurial classes and around the world. It was the first book Greg said I should read when I hit rock bottom, and it changed the way I looked at everything I did in business.

Together, these books keep me willing to be vulnerable while working in a more comfortable, data-driven approach to looking at my business. I highly recommend keeping both of those books close by.

Identity Threat

Another challenge business owners face when we start working on ATV leadership together is conceding failures. While most leaders readily admit past failures, they often push back against admitting failures in real time.

But this is what it takes to find a leadership role that is effective while not forcing you to pretend you're someone you're not all day. Brian Scudamore is just one example of a highly successful business leader who has not only overcome failure but has also actually embraced it as a key component of his identity. The C-suite is filled with many more. Here's the truth: if leaders are both effective and fulfilled, they're practicing ATV leadership, even if they don't know it.

So why is it so hard for so many of us to achieve such an outlook?

As humans, we've been born and bred to believe in better, better, better—the best we can be. Whether it's Keto and Paleo diets, milligrams of melatonin, or Mickey Mouse, we're bombarded with advice on how to eat better, sleep better, or even how to have a better time at Disney World. So our identities are naturally tied up in a one-way train, whistling toward whatever our personal best might be as defined by society or others. Who wants to jump off that train? Not me.

So when failure or potential failure starts whipping up, threatening derailment, we find distractions. We search for new recipes, new Amazon purchases, new Instagram posts. It's just like entrepreneurs do when we chase the next bright and shiny thing.

Mark Manson, the author of *The Subtle Art of Not Giving a F*ck,* calls this

"Manson's Law of Avoidance."[16] As he explains, it holds that "[t]he more something threatens your identity, the more you will avoid doing it."[17]

In other words, when something might change how we view ourselves and how we believe ourselves to be, the more we'll procrastinate about ever doing it.

"The crazy thing about Manson's Law is that it can apply to both good and bad things in one's life," Manson writes. "Making a million dollars can threaten your identity just as much as losing all your money. Becoming a famous rock star can threaten your identity just as much as losing your job. This is why people are often so afraid of success—for the exact same reason they're afraid of failure—it threatens who they are and what they know now."[18] It reminds me of the scene in the first Matrix movie when the Neo character is given the choice of picking either the Red Pill or the Blue Pill. One pill will allow you to see the brutal reality of how things really are, while the other pill will allow you to keep your head in the sand.

As you'll see in Chapter 4, the ATV process isn't complicated. It fits nicely into the simple four-part test that can help you improve your mind-set, leadership, and goal setting. It's the emotional part that's hard—the commitment to being authentic, transparent, and vulnerable around people you're not used to being that way around.

Authenticity: Getting Down With Your Bad Self
As we discussed in Chapter 1, shifting mind-set is the first step to making the complex simple. In order to reach the level of authenticity that allows us to become successful leaders, we must get real with our true selves first. What is your mind-set right now? Mind-set is what fuels success.

To truly discover your current, authentic mind-set, ask yourself these questions:
- What isn't working for me?
- What do I want to see happen?
- What is my greatest fear?
- What is my deepest self-doubt?
- What am I doing now that once worked for me, that no longer works for me? (Remember, progress only occurs when we are willing to let go of what was and replace it with what could be.)

Recently, I worked with six CEOs who hired me because they were part of a mastermind group trying to untangle the top five percent of issues tying up their lives and why their businesses weren't growing and why their relationships were suffering. When we went around the room a couple of times, I was getting surface answers: "It's the economy," "My spouse doesn't understand me," "My kids continually take my time and effort and attention."

I didn't accept these answers. I asked why multiple times. "Tell me more," I said repeatedly. I was ATV with them, and they were ATV with me, slowly. It took them really down into the depths of their soul. That's where the growth took place. One CEO (we'll call him Jeff) was talking about his relationship with his dad. He was never good enough for his dad; he never had enough revenue in the business. We started to peel away the layers of the onion of Jeff's life. As a group, we identified that he was super successful and that his revenue was awesome and that his marriage was to be admired and his parenting skills were solid. And I said to him, "Why don't we call your dad, and I will third-party validate how awesome you're doing and how you're living up to a lot of the core values you learned in his household, and a lot of the important takeaways you've gotten from the world." Jeff paused and he said to me, "I'd love to call him. But he's been dead for over a decade."

Jeff realized that the emptiness inside of himself—the most vulnerable hole within his soul—was there because he was trying to please a ghost. And then he started to shift. Then he started to move. Then he started to pivot into more positive language tracks and putting away the ghosts of the past. That's ATV at work.

Every healthy relationship with employees, customers, prospective clients, and significant others requires authenticity. Stick with it, and you'll soon discover hope. As you feel that hope build—that feeling of excitement for the future that we all have when we first get into entrepreneurship—that's your body telling you you're on the right track to rediscover the passion and purpose you had when you went into business in the first place.

Your "Why" And Your Ikigai

Over time, however, as we get deeper into entrepreneurship and the pieces of growing a business that we either don't like, aren't good at, or both, our excitement fades. Our business becomes a job. It owns us. We spend only a small amount of time doing the tasks we love to do and excel at. Over time, that excitement can disappear completely.

The good news is there's a solution. The great news is the solution is ATV. Specifically, remember that the "A" in ATV stands for authenticity. To reignite that fire, we must pursue something we authentically desire in a way that allows us to be our true, authentic selves.

We must find and identify a purpose for what we do that energizes us—the trendy but elusive concept that has become the centerpiece of much corporate leadership coaching. Once we've shed the layers of our inauthentic selves, we can begin to define our "why" and begin to identify the illusive purpose in both our business and personal lives. In other words, identifying our "why" will help us move forward much more authentically in everything we do.

The idea of "finding your 'why'" was popularized by the author, Simon Sinek, who in 2009, literally wrote the book on purpose: *Start with Why: How Great Leaders Inspire Everyone to Take Action.*[19] I should note here that Sinek coached me for a while, so I'm a bit biased, but when I finally broke through to identify and incorporate my purpose into what I do, everything in my life improved. I should also note that it took me two years to figure out the two words of "my why," even working with Sinek and using his tools and techniques. (Those two words? Improve lives. That is "my why.") But if you have struggled to identify your "why" up to this point, you're not alone. As Sinek explains, your "why" is your reason for getting out of bed in the morning.[20] I want to improve lives. If I get out of bed, I can do that. If not, I can't. So, on the days when I feel tired, I remind myself that the only way to change lives is to get up and get moving. It works every time.

In Japan, this sense of purpose is known as ikigai (pronounced ee-key-guy). It takes the concept of your "why" one step forward to help you identify a more tangible application of the seemingly intangible concept. Simply put, you find your *ikigai* at the intersection of what you are good at, what you love, what the world needs, and what you can be paid for. As Hector Garcia, the coauthor with Francesc Miralles of *Ikigai: The Japanese Secret to a Long and Happy Life*, explains, "[j]ust as humans have lusted after objects and money since the dawn of time, other humans have felt dissatisfaction at the relentless pursuit of money and fame and have instead focused on something bigger than their own material wealth. This has over the years been described using many different words and practices, but always hearkening back to the central core of meaningfulness in life."[21]

For visual learners, the following image can help. If you've struggled to find the energy and excitement you had when you first pursued entrepreneurship, it's possible that you've strayed from your "why," your ikigai, and could benefit from slowing down a bit to find it again. In other words, your systems and processes might need improvement, but your best next step is to slow down and work on reconnecting with your greater purpose. When you do, you may realize that it is unnecessary to improve on some of the systems and processes you might be inclined to improve on because they involve activities that aren't aligned with the bigger picture.

Slow Down

There's no Autobahn to this intersection of what you're good at and what you love doing—not to mention what the world needs and what you can be paid for. The only shortcut to success is to take the "longcut" to discovering your *ikigai*. It's the best way to fill your days with activities that bring you energy, and to reignite the energy you had when you started your business. These days, I often have more energy at the end of the day than I do at the beginning. That's what living in your *ikigai* does. But like I mentioned, it took me two years to find my *ikigai* of improving lives even with the best coaching and training available. It was a struggle to figure it out—a lot of false stops and starts. And it developed over time. This is not a one-time exercise or something that's going to happen overnight.

Now I bring my *ikigai* to everything I do. It crosses all spheres of my world—business, family, and personal. Whether it's my son or my client, I approach everyone similarly by asking questions, discovering "aha!" moments, and allowing them to leave the conversation in a better place. My ikigai not only helps me say yes to projects that align with my purpose but even more importantly it helps me say no to those that don't.

I have developed the mind-set of improving lives, and I take it everywhere I go.

Many academics are prescriptive about what we should or should not do, and doubly theoretical. They miss out on the long, iterative process of tracking down many different aspects of ourselves until something really sticks. People get wrapped up in the "American Idol" thought process because on the surface, it looks like the performer—let's call him John—just sings for three celebrity judges. He's amazing! His success is so fast! And he gets a million-dollar record contract! That's the story we tell ourselves. But it's not true.

The reality is, John's been studying music since he was age three. He's now eighteen. For fifteen years, he's practiced his craft at twenty different instruments. People miss that because they're looking for that rocket ship to success. It's an iterative process.

Another way to think of *ikigai* is as a beloved cast-iron skillet. It takes years to cure the skillet with your own cooking—your most prized recipes, your own seasonings, the remnants of dinner parties are all in there. Over the course of time, it becomes well-worn, well-honed. And that's when it works.

Ikigai And Imposter Syndrome

As *Psychology Today* explains, Imposter Syndrome is "[a] psychological phenomenon in which people are unable to internalize their accomplishments."[22]

Megan Dalla-Camina writes more on this topic in a recent *Psychology Today* article.[23] "The imposter syndrome is a psychological term referring to a pattern of behavior where people doubt their accomplishments and have a persistent, often internalized fear of being exposed as a fraud," she writes.

> Not an actual disorder, the term was coined by clinical psychologists Pauline Clance and Suzanne Imes in 1978, when they found that despite having adequate external evidence of accomplishments, people with imposter syndrome remained convinced that they don't deserve the success they have.

> They call their success luck or good timing, and dismiss it as others' believing they were better, more intelligent, and more competent than they actually are. And while yes, early research from the psychologists' work focused on high-achieving women, the syndrome has actually been found to impact men and women in roughly equal numbers.

> We all suffer from it. I've known the most senior men who struggle with it day in day out. General managers running billion-dollar companies. Speakers who command audiences in the thousands. Powerful men who still wonder if what they are doing is good enough, or if they are about to be found out for being an imposter.[24]

Dalla-Camina goes on:

> You know how it goes: You get the promotion at work, and your inner narrative is that they must have been short on candidates. Your business has a great win, and you tell yourself that it was sheer chance that the client found you (and they mustn't have looked too far and wide). You are getting ready to give a presentation, and you secretly think that you're about to be found out for how hopeless you really are. Or you're sitting in a big meeting and you just know that the boss will walk in any minute, tap you on the shoulder, and tell you they have finally realized that you really aren't qualified for the job (even though you're the most experienced person in the room). It can be completely derailing.
>
> We know from the research that imposter syndrome is in large part a reaction to certain circumstances or situations. So while you may feel fully confident speaking to a group of more junior people, addressing your peers could completely undo you. Or you could be fine at work, but having to speak up at the local school meeting? Forget about it. A tendency toward perfectionism, fear of failure, continually undermining one's achievements (trekking up Mount Kilimanjaro? Oh, it was nothing!) are all indicators that you might be prone. And it can be debilitating, causing stress, anxiety, low self-confidence, shame, and in some cases, even depression.[25]

When I work with entrepreneurs on developing their *ikigai*, we frequently run up against Imposter Syndrome. Take my *ikigai* of improving lives, for example. My ikigai tells me that I need to build a business and live my family and personal life in such a way that I'm consistently improving lives.

When I write that down on paper, I still sometimes feel butterflies in my stomach, thinking *Who am I to be changing people's lives?* The nature of finding your *ikigai* is such that it pushes us out of our comfort zone toward activities that are bigger than ourselves. And the truth is that while my coaching ends up changing lives, it's the action that my clients take that ultimately leads them forward, not any magic words from me. I push them. I guide them. I help them stay accountable and consistent. But, really, *they're* the ones who actually change their lives.

Just like me, virtually every client of mine who works on identifying their *ikigai* has this "Who am I?" moment. They have it frequently. When our *ikigai* is so important to us, that feeling is natural—especially after struggling for so long. After all, if you hire a coach because you're working A hundred hours a week, haven't seen your kids in who knows when, and can't get your team members to perform consistently, it's natural to doubt yourself.

I wish I could pull up a chair next to yours or jump on a Zoom call with you right now because this is something I like to say when looking at someone face to face. But that's not how books operate so I'll just say it. I've worked with a lot of people. I've been there myself, sitting on the curb, $600,000 in debt and feeling like a complete failure. All of what's going on right now doesn't define you. It's not who you are. It's just your current circumstances.

There's no way I thought I could help other people change their lives back in 2006. I couldn't even run my own life. But I could. I can. I have. And you can, too. If you're feeling butterflies, that's your brain doubting yourself. That's natural. That's your body telling you to push forward, even if your brain is telling you to back down.

Turn Imposter Syndrome From Suck To Success

If Imposter Syndrome is normal and happens to nearly everyone, what's the solution? First, the solution is to accept it, anticipate it, and look for the warning signs. Two common warning signs are butterflies and comparisons. The butterflies in your gut are a sign you're on the right track toward something meaningful. For comparisons, consider when you're at a dinner party or networking event, or scrolling on social media, and you anticipate seeing people bragging about all the success they're achieving. If you find yourself comparing their success stories to your worst moments or deepest insecurities, that's Imposter Syndrome.

It doesn't matter your station in life. It doesn't matter how much revenue you have. It doesn't matter how many awards you've won. Nearly all of us have suffered from Imposter Syndrome and continue to suffer from it. For example, in elementary school, I was terrible at math. I was really good at English and writing compositions. But because I was so bad at math, all I did was beat myself up about it. I thought everyone else had math figured out but me. That's part of what happens with Imposter Syndrome. I was making assumptions about everyone else that weren't true. Just like when we see what appears to be someone who has it all figured out in person or on social media. We're seeing a surface-level snapshot and comparing it to our biggest struggles and insecurities. We don't know what's going on behind closed doors. We don't know if their business is built on a pile of debt, or if their marriage is struggling, or if their health is poor. We just know they got a new car and are taking an expensive vacation. But we do know everything in our life that sucks.

Most of the entrepreneurs I'm now working with suffer from some sort of Imposter Syndrome. Many times, it comes from not having all the answers to the questions that need to be answered between their present circumstances and the business and life they want to live. With me, I didn't know how I was going to change lives. I needed to do a lot of work to figure out exactly how I was going to be able to do that. I had way more questions than answers. That caused me to wonder whether I could even do it.

As I kept going, I realized the gap between my present circumstances and the future I wanted was not one monstrous gap. It was a series of smaller gaps I needed to overcome. I just couldn't see those smaller steps at the time. I could only see the big gap, and that's where my Imposter Syndrome really started beating me up.

When we pursue our *ikigai,* we will naturally see the big gap and not the small gaps that lead us there because we don't have all the answers at the beginning. When that happens, we need to remind ourselves that it's OK not to have all the answers right away. We don't even know all the *questions* when we start. We just know what we want our destination to look like. Part of the process is to try things, have them not work, and iterate from there. Trying and failing should be championed, not criticized. And it doesn't mean we can't do it. It just means we need to try something else.

Finding Strength In Vulnerability

As we turn our Imposter Syndrome from something that sucks to something that pushes us toward success, we must be careful. We will begin to feel vulnerable, exposed. When that happens, we will generally fall into one of two groups. One group takes on a "fake it 'til you make it" mentality. They push forward pretending to know what they're doing and to have all the answers. The other group is the "willing to be a little vulnerable" group. That group will admit they don't have all the answers but move forward anyway, willing to ask for help and figure things out along the way.

Entrepreneurs who fall into the "fake it 'til you make it" group almost always continue to struggle. In fact, it's the "fake it 'til you make it" mentality that often leads people into a world of suck in the first place. They pretend they know what they're doing. They don't get advice or direction from others. And they end up making a big mess.

Entrepreneurs who fall into the "willing to be a little vulnerable" group almost always end up better off. It's a bit counterintuitive, of course, but having a healthy vulnerability is one of the best strength-building exercises you can do to achieve success.

This brings me to an important point about ATV leadership. Remember, the "A" stands for authentic, the "T" stands for transparent, and the "V" stands for vulnerable. That's what it takes to be a world-class leader. Notice that nowhere in the structure does it mention having advanced degrees, being a smooth talker, or having thirty years of experience. If you can be authentic, transparent, and vulnerable, you can be an impactful leader. Most leaders don't object to the authenticity part. It's not that uncomfortable to work on being more authentic. But transparency and vulnerability are a whole other ballgame. Let's start with vulnerability.

One of the best ways to find strength in vulnerability is to pair vulnerability with mentorship. Of course, you can get mentorship in many ways, including books, podcasts, group memberships, or even coaching. The information and accountability you receive through mentorship helps you grow your knowledge and have accountability to do the hard work it takes to push through obstacles.

Vulnerability Is Not A Four-Letter Word

As we finish up the deep dive into vulnerability, I wanted to highlight one important truth—vulnerability is uncomfortable. It's been uncomfortable for years. It's been ingrained in us since childhood. Once upon a time, we viewed being vulnerable as being soft and weak at the knees. A vulnerable person was a lily-livered coward who would kowtow to the slightest challenge that came their way.

As you move forward, let me emphasize that, as Brian Scudamore proved with 1-800-GOT-JUNK?, the opposite is in fact true. Today, vulnerability is a sought-after attribute as leaders begin to realize that learning to embrace and even seek vulnerability is a wonderful step toward extraordinary entrepreneurship. Indeed, "vulnerability is the birthplace of innovation, creativity, and change," writes author Brené Brown.[26] Pick up any of Brown's incredible books and keep them close by. She has almost single-handedly reversed the vilification of vulnerability in several books, not just in *Dare to Lead* but also in *Daring Greatly: How the Courage to Be Vulnerable Transforms the Way We Live, Love, Parent, and Lead; The Gifts of Imperfection: Let Go of Who You Think You're Supposed to Be and Embrace Who You Are*, and many others. If she writes something, read it.

Regarding potential weakness, she makes clear: "Yes, we are totally exposed when we are vulnerable. Yes, we are in the torture chamber that we call uncertainty. And, yes, we're taking a huge emotional risk when we allow ourselves to be vulnerable. But there's no equation where taking risks, braving uncertainty, and opening ourselves up to emotional exposure equals weakness." [27]

But Brown continues and debunks the various myths:
1. "Vulnerability is a Weakness"
2. "I Don't Do Vulnerability"
3. "Vulnerability is Letting It All Hang Out"
4. "We Can Go It Alone"[28]

The opposite is true of all these long-held beliefs. Long-held beliefs that keep you from being vulnerable are what make you weak. Vulnerability makes you stronger. And we all do vulnerability. We all have the capacity to share the right amount of vulnerability—and we all depend on each other to use vulnerability to our advantage.

Suck vs. Success

The only way to get unstuck and go from suck to success in your business is to innovate. So many entrepreneurs get wrapped up in "What worked for me before" and "It should work for me now." That's not how it goes. I've had clients struggle deeply with "What's wrong with me?"

The better approach is, "This isn't working for me. What can I do differently? How can I go from a reactive mind-set, which was so wrapped up in fight or flight, to a creative mind-set, which is going to open up creativity, open up innovation, and open up change?"

As I write this, I'm working with a client who wanted to stop running her business full-time. She felt very vulnerable about standing in front of her team, telling them she wanted to move from CEO to chairwoman. She was wrapped up in what she perceived as a weakness. So, we pivoted her out of that, and her business is growing. Her leadership is behind her, and she's begun the process to shift to an even higher level of leadership as chairwoman. Her team is putting new processes in place and taking more responsibility and ownership of their roles. And she's enjoying her life more. But it took a moment of great vulnerability to stand up and admit she wasn't fulfilled by her role as CEO to make it happen.

See-Through Transparency

So what about the other piece of the ATV puzzle, the "T" for transparency? Like vulnerability, transparency requires overcoming long-held beliefs about what it means to be transparent as a leader. Being transparent helps you build deeper relationships with your team and give them important context to the work you ask them to do.

One of the best examples of someone whose transparency helped unlock progress beyond what she dreamed possible is a client we'll call Nicole. She confided in me that she had quit years of heavy drinking. She felt great, but she also found herself hiding everything: her emotions, her secret stash of dark chocolate, her Netflix binges when she was supposed to be working.

Nicole had even pilfered a few things in her pockets from the local gourmet store—not because she didn't have the money but because she was hooked on hiding. Until she opened up to me, she had kept her struggles a secret. She was putting on a facade in public. Nobody knew what she was secretly dealing with.

Nicole's hardly alone. As much as humans depend on each other, we all have a tendency to protect ourselves by stashing away things we're not proud of. But in order for us to go from suck to success, we must be fully transparent with the people who matter most to us and with ourselves. Of course, this doesn't mean we should broadcast details about our private lives to the world. The level of transparency we reveal to some people is different than we reveal to others. For example, we have a duty to ourselves and those closest to us to explore and share our personal struggles. Otherwise, they can't help and support us, and the pressure on ourselves will build. Likewise, we have a duty to our team members to share the inside out of business operations so they can know how to perform their tasks and support us as leaders.

Jack Stack's book *The Great Game of Business: The Only Sensible Way to Run a Company* demonstrates financial transparency and open book management. As he summarizes, "[t]he idea behind this concept is that when employees gain a better understanding of how the organization is run, they become empowered by this knowledge and it gives them 'a dog in the fight,' so to speak. This is because people will fight for that which they have helped create, and because they want to understand how their contributions correlate to success. Often employees see their share of the work in isolation and never know the direct tie to how much they are helping (or hurting) their employer. When this information is unknown, people will assume that their hard work is enabling the company to make a great deal of money, of which they see little. As owners and managers, we know this isn't the case."[29]

In my previous career at Diversified Industrial Staffing, I embraced Jack Stack's methods, posting all our financial numbers. No more surprises. By every Sunday, my accounting team needed to provide our invoicing, which we'd compare against our run rate for costs. In the weeks we made money, we celebrated. In the weeks we lost money, we talked about what happened. It was uncomfortable for me to publish that information. I was embarrassed by some of it, concerned that other parts of it would create animosity. But keeping everything hidden hadn't worked, so I didn't really have much to lose. I now know from appearing on the *Inc. 5000* list so many times that my concerns, while reasonable, were misplaced. (They also kept me and my team hyperfocused on profitable revenue growth.)

One of the more immediate benefits of posting the numbers was that it allowed us to pivot in real time. We didn't have to wait until monthly numbers were finalized midway through the following month to evaluate our performance. When we were able to do that in real time, it was beneficial for our employees. They knew where we stood as a company at any given time. We talked as a group and we always knew, for example, that the weeks before, during, and after the holiday season were slow for our business. But we'd budget for these slow quarters.

For any leader who is hiring and managing a new team, the effects of financial transparency are profound. "When people are given a sense of control, they understand that they are responsible and can't put the blame on others," Stack writes. "This autonomy creates accountability and a feeling of pride for an individual who knows they have helped create a successful outcome. Relatedness refers to shared goals. At the center of open-book management is the ideal of rallying around a common cause and everyone assessing how they can do their part to accomplish the goal."

What ATV Means For You And Your Teams

When it comes to leadership, there is no doubt in my mind that you will achieve far more success with ATV than an MBA over the long term. I have nothing against the MBA. It's a fine degree. But I'd much rather have two people with ATV and no MBA on my team than ten people with MBAs but no ATV. The ATV leaders will get much better results and build a much healthier culture in an organization than MBAs who don't lead through ATV.

Once you've learned to be authentic, transparent, and vulnerable, you'll discover how much more your teams will follow you because you'll be more believable on a very cellular level. Think about it. When someone's lying to us or someone's giving us partial truths, or half-truths, or even lying by omission by not sharing the truth, then we experience that on a very raw level, and it causes us not to trust them.

And because we don't trust them, we're not going to follow them because we only want to follow leaders we can believe in. The opposite of that, then, is to be authentic, transparent, invulnerable.

ATV Is Always The Answer

Before moving into setting intentions, I want to make one more note. As I was writing this book, the world came screeching to a halt as a result of the COVID-19 pandemic. Businesses were forced to shut down temporarily; many closed their doors for good. Of the businesses that reopened, they didn't open back to how they operated pre-pandemic in so many ways.

Even my business got blindsided. My clients faced uncertainty. Keynotes and company training sessions were canceled. Conferences around the world went virtual or were postponed.

What do you do when the world around you falls into chaos? That's the beauty of ATV: it's timeless. It works in good economies and bad. It works with big budgets and small ones. It works when the wind is at your back or when you're in the middle of a hurricane. It's natural to want to shift during times of uncertainty. But that's the worst time to ditch ATV leadership. It's when you need it the most.

For example, as I write these words, I'm imploring one client to be real with her employees on a consistent basis. From the realities of the company's finances to the feelings she's experiencing, I've emphasized that her team will be more understanding and supportive if she demonstrates the authenticity, transparency, and vulnerability that has helped her during more stable times.

I encouraged her to share the process of applying for government programs put in place to stabilize the economy, such as the Paycheck Protection Program (PPP) and the Economic Injury Disaster Loan (EIDL) program. So she shared with her team that she applied but wasn't sure whether they would be getting government funding. She shared even when she didn't have an update. She and her leadership team updated their staff on a consistent basis on where they stood. Even when she didn't have an update, her team felt cared for.

I also asked her to begin every team meeting by being real and vulnerable: "I just want to let you know that I'm thinking of all of you in these tough times and that I'm here for you. Please, if anybody needs to reach out, if anybody needs to talk, I'm here. I want you to know that I miss seeing your faces in the office. I miss interacting with you as a team. And please know that you and your families are always in my thoughts."

She started this process with daily emails. Then she dug deep and started to share her daily updates on videos so her team could not only hear her words but also see her face and feel her emotions. That was getting ATV! Lead with vulnerability, lead with transparency, lead with authenticity. When you do, you validate the moment and build deeper relationships with your team. When times are chaotic, it's especially important to overcommunicate on what you know and don't know. In this case, my client told her team:

> I filled out all the government forms and now we're in a wait-and-hold period. I assume we get the money, but it's out of our hands. Here are our next steps. If we don't get the money, here's our plan. Overall, here's where we stand. If anybody has any questions about the PPP or EIDL, please reach out and let me know. I'm happy to talk you through where we stand.

> There's a lot of uncertainty right now. There's a lot of change going on in our world. Please know that I'm embracing that as much as I possibly can. But like you, having to deal with change has been thrust upon us through COVID. It is difficult. So I'm doing the best I can with what I've got. If anybody has an idea or anybody sees opportunities that I'm not seeing, by all means, as a leader, I want to encourage you to reach out to me and let me know what you see so I can do the best job for all of us.

That openness is so important to share, especially when we don't know where we're going. If you're ever in doubt, remember that ATV is always the answer.

Insights
- Take the journey and discover your "why," your ikigai.
- Failure is a lesson learned, a necessary step along your pathway to learning and growing.
- Embrace ATV in all aspects of business and life.
- Nearly everyone suffers from some form of Imposter Syndrome. You are not alone.

Questions For Reflection
- Where does the Law of Avoidance show up in your life? What threatens your identity and what are you doing to avoid it?
- With whom in your life can you show up and be more ATV with? (Write a list.)
- What is your current authentic mind-set? Are you willing to get rid of behaviors that no longer serve you well?
- What is your life's purpose, your deepest "why"?

Action Steps
- Recognize when your Imposter Syndrome becomes activated and develop replacement language to improve your self-talk.
- Take the risk and begin to live your ikigai.
- Recognize and embrace failure as part of the learning process. Iterate and learn through it.

Additional Resources
Brown, Brené. *The Gifts of Imperfection: Let Go of Who You Think You're Supposed to Be and Embrace Who You Are.* Center City, Minnesota: Hazelden Publishing, 2010.

Brown, Brené. Daring Greatly: *How the Courage to Be Vulnerable Transforms the Way We Live, Love, Parent, and Lead.* New York: Avery, 2012.

Brown, Brené. *Dare to Lead: Brave Work. Tough Conversations. Whole Hearts.* New York: Random House, 2018.

Collins, Jim. *Good to Great: Why Some Companies Make the Leap . . . and Others Don't.* New York: HarperCollins, 2001.

Garcia, Hector and Francesc Miralles. *Ikigai: The Japanese Secret to a Long and Happy Life.* London: Penguin Books, 2017.

Manson, Mark. *Everything Is F*cked: A Book about Hope.* New York: HarperCollins, 2019.

Scudamore, Brian. *WTF?! (Willing to Fail): How Failure Can Be Your Key to Success.* Lioncrest Publishing, 2018.

Sinek, Simon. *Start with Why: How Great Leaders Inspire Everyone to Take Action.* New York: Penguin Group, 2009.

Stack, Jack. *The Great Game of Business: The Only Sensible Way to Run a Company.* New York: Crown Business, 1992.

Also visit ExtraordinaryAdvisors.com for more exclusive coaching tips.

Chapter 3

Setting An Intention, Not An Expectation

"If you want something you have never had, you must be willing to do something you have never done."
— Thomas Jefferson

More than four million people are tuning into *Shark Tank*, the award-winning reality TV show that gives budding entrepreneurs a chance to secure investments from some of the best entrepreneurs in the world, known to the audience as the "sharks." The sharks have a history of success in business and frequently turn small businesses into multi-million-dollar enterprises after they appear on the show. From the Scrub Daddy ($75 million in revenue in three years) to Bubba's Q Boneless Baby Back Ribs (projected to cook up $200 million in lifetime sales), *Shark Tank* has elevated many products to international distribution and launched several entrepreneurial careers.

Part of my fascination with the show is in one shark in particular, Barbara Corcoran. Barbara is one of the best examples of extraordinary entrepreneurship in many ways. As fans of *Shark Tank* have learned, she got straight Ds in high school and college and jumped from job to job, twenty in all before she was twenty-three years old. But then Corcoran decided on her own terms to make the complex simple, quitting her waitressing job, borrowing $1,000, and starting a simple real estate office that she sold in 2001 for $66 million.

Corcoran is also a prime example of setting better goals by focusing on intentions rather than expectations. While other sharks on *Shark Tank* appear to be more rigid in how they approach deals, Corcoran is one of the more flexible and open-minded sharks. The deals she makes are creative but opportunistic, and her new business partners are undoubtedly better off because of it.

Why Intentions Beat Expectations Every Time

There's a tendency in business to expect good things to happen, to lead with a positive mind-set and expect good things to follow. But like we learned in Chapter 1 that naked positive thinking will only lull you into inaction, setting expectations instead of intentions can set you up for failure when it comes to making progress in business. As you'll learn in the next several pages:

- intentions are flexible,
- expectations are static,
- intentions can pivot off new information,
- expectations are win-lose scenarios,
- intentions create abundance and opportunity, and
- expectations create very narrow pathways.

There's no better example of the power of setting intentions instead of expectations than the challenges brought about by the COVID-19 pandemic that started in late 2019. In that case, the entire world had developed an expectation about what business and life looked like, and rightfully so—business and life had generally followed the same script for the past 100 years to that point. Then, sometime in the beginning of 2020, as disease and fear spread, countries all around the world shut down. Stock markets crashed. Businesses closed, many for good. People's incomes plummeted. It was tragic, to say the least.

If you look deeper into the aftermath of the first six months of the pandemic, however, you will notice that two groups of people or companies seemed to get through relatively unscathed—either bouncing back quickly after a short struggle or barely experiencing a struggle at all.

The first group consisted mostly of larger companies considered "essential" such as those that sold groceries or household goods. You don't have to look far to learn about those companies. Companies, such as Amazon and other online retailers, thrived during the COVID-19 pandemic by offering different retail shopping experiences than most people were used to. People who never would have thought to order groceries and some other categories of goods online shifted to online buying by necessity. Many of those people discovered how safe, secure, and convenient it is to shop online. Some will never go back to the old way of buying.

The second group of people and companies barely made headlines, though, because you can't put them in a neat category like "consumer goods companies." I think of this second group as intention-driven people and businesses. Why? Because the common characteristic you will notice across this group is the ability to pivot to achieve the same desired result they were seeking, but just in a different way.

To be clear, I'm not talking about price gougers who bought up all the hand sanitizer and tried to rip off the public by reselling it for exorbitant prices online. I'm talking about the people and companies that pivoted to doing business differently than they had before while achieving the same or better results.

I'm talking about healthcare providers who pivoted to telemedicine to continue to serve patients. They used technology to adjust how they provided care to patients, in many cases with better results for both patients and the medical practice. For example, virtual consultations allowed people to consult an expert to determine fit without having to take time off work or expose themselves to other patients. They also allowed medical practices to have all decision makers attend appointments together. Spouses could attend virtual appointments with each other. Adult children could get more involved in the care of their elderly parents. Although many facilities were closed to some patients, many of the providers who pivoted to telemedicine continued to serve their patients while even improving access to and the speed of care.

And I'm talking about the clothing manufacturers who started creating masks. They intended to make a profit and employ people through manufacturing and distributing clothes. When everything shut down, they shifted to making a profit and employing people through manufacturing and distributing masks. (And, of course, some were in a position to even donate some or all of those masks to worthy recipients.)

I'm talking about the distilleries that started producing hand sanitizer. They entered 2020 intending to make a profit and employ people through manufacturing and distributing alcohol. When everything shut down, they shifted to making a profit and employing people through manufacturing and distributing hand sanitizer. (And, again, some were in a position to even donate hand sanitizer to worthy recipients.)

And I'm talking about the public speakers who pivoted to online learning, individual coaching and investing in their audience without expectation of immediate payment. They intended to make a profit and spread messages by flying around the country, jumping on stages, and sharing their story with hundreds of people at conferences or companies. When everything shut down, they shifted to making a profit virtually and through more individualized attention.

All of these companies had one thing in common: they pivoted to take advantage of all the tools at their disposal to identify and fill demand, even if that meant using raw materials to create different products or completely shifting how they deliver services. Coach Cameron Herold recently reflected in a Facebook post on a conversation he'd had with a COO about how technology impacted the business community's ability to shift during the COVID-19 pandemic.[30] He mentioned how the availability of Wi-Fi, video conferencing, team communication channels like Slack, and other technologies helped the world avoid the complete destruction of the global economy. And he said companies likely would have opened up sooner to avoid collapse—putting consumers and staff at risk—if not for technology. But technology allowed many companies to go remote that never could have if the pandemic occurred even twenty years earlier.

Setting intentions rather than expectations will create a subtle but important mind-set shift that causes your reaction to adversity to be solution focused rather than problem focused. Solution-focused entrepreneurs quickly shift to identify other ways to achieve desired results when adversity strikes. Problem-focused entrepreneurs often spend too much time looking to blame or making excuses for not being able to achieve the results they desire.

Setting intentions was a lesson I learned early on when digging myself out of debt. I still remember my first intention: to find a more profitable business. That was it. My margins were razor thin at Diversified Industrial Staffing. Any one challenge could quickly shift us to the red. So my team and I set an intention to find a more profitable focus in the staffing world that had stronger margins than our original focus. This helped us pivot and go after a very niche segment of the staffing world we discovered that allowed us to charge more and get paid faster. We found that inflection point where there was an increased demand and a diminished supply for skilled trades talent around the Midwest. And it all started by setting a simple intention that, if achieved, would help me solve all my other financial problems both in and outside of the business.

Over the rest of this chapter, we'll talk about how and why you can set yourself up to make progress in any environment by setting intentions rather than expectations.

Blockbuster Or Bust?

While Barbara Corcoran doesn't overtly come out and say it, we don't need to do much digging to see how much of her success resulted because of her natural tendency to set intentions—not expectations. For example, with respect to rejection, she has said, "I consider your rejection a lucky charm, because everything great that ever happened in my life came on the heels of failure."[31] In other words, for Corcoran, failure is a sign of something great to come. All she needs to do is pause, pivot, and head toward that next great achievement.

Beyond Corcoran's view of failure, her history in business is packed with examples of achieving things in different ways. For example, in an effort to differentiate herself from other real estate agents, she spent her company's first profits on a video marketing initiative. Her idea was to put all of her apartments for sale onto VHS and mail the video tapes to prospects. This would allow potential customers the opportunity to shop for apartments from the comfort of their own homes, like we do today. Previously, interested renters would need to carve out time into their schedule to view apartments in person. Corcoran thought that if they could review the apartments via videotape, they would save time and money, while giving her an edge over her competition.

Unfortunately, it turned out to be a disaster. She was ahead of her time, and logistics removed much of the benefit of her idea. By the time the video was sent to an interested real estate buyer, often the listing had been sold, making the videotape obsolete—marketing junk mail. The idea was dead on arrival.

But the internet was in its infancy at that time, so Corcoran decided to post some of the videos and images online and then send those webpages to potential buyers. *That* experiment worked, and within two days she had buyers from London purchasing one of her New York apartments. She knew she had hit upon a winning marketing formula of using videos and images instead of in-person tours to sell homes—just as she *intended* but not as she may have *expected*.

Energy In Intention

The challenge many entrepreneurs have with setting intentions instead of expectations is the fact that the shift from expectations to intentions is a subtle one. Most of our lives revolve around expectations. We expect a good education. We expect to have a good career. We expect to get married and have children. We expect to retire with the second home of our dreams. But expectations are win-lose scenarios. They are right or wrong situations, and we often get stuck in a bad one because we expect it to work out.

One of the best examples of how impactful it is to make the subtle shift from expectations to intentions is the typical person feeling stuck in a toxic workplace. An expectation-driven person hangs on far too long, complaining at work or home and eventually putting in just enough effort to *not* get fired. Their entire life is miserable. But they don't switch because they expect something to change at that job. An intention-driven person hangs on just long enough to find a better job. They intend to have a supportive work environment somewhere. If their current situation isn't providing one, they'll find one that does.

Expectation-driven people say, "If I want what I want, the way I want it to happen, it's to be expected." But what if it doesn't happen? They think something is wrong and end up disappointed and frustrated. That will impact their ability to creatively problem solve when those inevitable things happen. When things inevitably don't happen the way we think they should, frustration rises and saps our energy. Specifically, it saps our problem-solving energy. It limits our creativity. It spirals, and to nowhere good.

If that sounds too specific to be hypothetical, it's because it is. That was me. I'm a recovering expectation junkie. I used to tell myself that if I just go to college, get my degree, and marry a pretty girl, then I'll just live a happy life. I'll be happy.

So my expectation was A (education); plus B (job); plus C (wife) equals D—happy life! And as we know, that doesn't happen. Those were tough lessons for me to learn along the way. But that was parental programming. My mom would often say, "Todd, if you go to school, you'll get a great job. You'll marry a pretty girl. Then you'll just be happy." And I experienced disappointment because I did all that and I wasn't happy. I am not bashing my mom or any other parent who is doing the best they can. In her case, my mom had only the best in mind for me. It was her expectation-laced delivery that caused me problems.

An intention, on the other hand, is something we want to happen and plan to do. But it's open-ended and makes us be open-minded and intentional. That thinking detaches us from the goal. It creates opportunities to learn along the way by staying curious, allowing us to focus on the present: "Where am I right now? Enjoying the process and freeing myself from the outcome, which is often seen as a win or a loss?" But by being detached from a specific outcome, we can adapt quickly and effectively along the journey because we are going to be emotionally invested in just reaching that goal. We can gain more energy along the way, and when that energy dips, we can return to the E-4 Process I'll share with you in the next chapter to recharge your batteries.

Making the subtle shift from expectations to intention isn't natural for many entrepreneurs, especially those of us who are more outcome focused than journey focused. By switching from expectations to intentions, we let go of specific outcomes and instead focus on the essence of our journey. The process of reaching becomes more important than the process of arriving. As entrepreneurs, we struggle with this. We're so goal driven.

When we are goal and outcome driven and keep getting pushed around by variables that are outside of our control, our energy drops precipitously. It can be all consuming. Personally, I only defined having a "successful" staffing company as one where I reached $20 million in revenue. (I never hit that number.) So by that definition, regardless of whether we made money, won awards, received accolades, or got out of debt, I would be considered a failure to an expectation-focused entrepreneur who defined $20 million in revenue as the metric to achieve success.

But by switching to intention from expectation, I was more focused on my journey. That focus helped me put in place success metrics that demonstrated positive momentum and achievement along the way. For example, we identified getting out of debt and pivoting into more profitable opportunities as two intentions early on. Those intentions caused me to change my hiring processes to position me to make those pivots to higher-margin work. It helped me avoid thinking there was only one way to achieve a goal and find an even better way to move forward.

The Men On The Moon

In the Apollo 13 mission, as the movie shares with us, the expectation of astronauts James Lovell and crew might have been for a flawless execution: "We're going to leave Earth. We're going to land on the moon and then we're going to leave the moon and we're to propel with our rockets back to Earth."[32] But we know that didn't happen. That's why it's so important that the team at NASA pursued their mission, like they do with all missions, with an intention mind-set rather than an expectation mind-set.

By setting intentions for a safe mission and return to Earth, Lovell and his crew were prepared for the unexpected challenges they faced during the mission. Here's what really happened with Apollo 13.

First, the explosion of an oxygen tank caused Apollo 13 to malfunction. The team needed to pivot. A moon landing wasn't possible. They had to abort. But Space Center Houston was very clear that a total failure of the mission was not an option. They needed to get the team home safely. There were several big problems, however. Most critically, the only remaining oxygen supply was designed to support two people for two days and the crew of three needed four days of oxygen to get home. In addition, power onboard was reduced, the cabin was cold and wet, and their water supply was limited. The crew needed the water not only to drink but also to cool the electronic circuits onboard. The team needed to improvise.

If you've watched the movie *Apollo 13* or remember when the actual mission happened, you know the crew ultimately made it back to Earth safely. Exactly how they did so is quite a bit beyond the scope of this book. But the approach the NASA engineers and the Apollo 13 crew took to repurpose equipment and adjust their plans throughout the process is exactly how the most successful entrepreneurs approach their business and personal lives.

I've yet to meet an entrepreneur who can honestly say that everything in their business regularly goes according to plan. In fact, it's even hard to think of single days during which everything goes according to plan. So if we're too rigid with setting goals, schedules, and how we walk into the office each day, we are not setting ourselves up for success.

So what's the answer? Setting intentions instead of expectations so we can be quick to adapt when we encounter the reality of our unpredictable days. We need to be creative in how we look at solving the problems we face. Like how the crew of Apollo 13 reimagined the supplies on the rocket ship to achieve their most important goal of making it home safely, what can we do to achieve our most important goals when things go wrong? Additionally, how can we avoid getting stuck in the flawed approach of not pivoting out of frustration that our original vision didn't go according to plan? We need to be disciplined in our approach, setting intentions from the start.

Suck vs. Success

We have to accept the uncertainty of our experience, which can be very difficult for all of us. I know because I struggle with it myself. Phrases of expectations sound like this: "It's not turning out as I expected."

The self-talk is "I have to," "I need to," "It should be this way," "She is supposed to do this," and "He is supposed to do that." Whereas intentional statements sound like "I want to," "I decided to," and "I choose to." Those are much more impactful, self-empowering statements.

Learning From Uncertainty And Change

I wrote an article in August 2020 while the country was still in the midst of the COVID-19 pandemic. I share it here because it's an important reminder that the world runs in cycles. While events like the pandemic are unique, what's not unique is that we will all face periods of uncertainty and change on a regular basis. We will run up against macroeconomic challenges like recessions, war, and pandemics. And we will run up against microeconomic challenges like health issues, relationship challenges, or the loss of key team members.

These lessons apply to any time of uncertainty and change. When you face them, I encourage you to come back and replace "2020" and "COVID-19" with the uncertainty you're facing. Then visit Chapter 4 to walk through the four-step process to move forward in strength.

Two words I am hearing lately in the business community are "uncertainty" and "change." Uncertainty in 2020 is easily attributable to the COVID-19 pandemic and its impact on the economy, the employee/employer working relationship, supply chain interruption, and more. Change, on the other hand, is constant in business. The need for change in business occurs with or without the presence of a pandemic. So, why is change so difficult for many of us? Procrastination.

For example, a CEO knows that his company should implement a new marketing campaign to drive new sales, yet he doesn't commit to spending the money and puts it off. Or a plant manager knows he needs to fire a toxic employee, but the plant manager cannot pull the trigger on their termination because "it's not the right time." These are decisions that significantly impact the business.

Business-changing decisions are deeply emotional, stressful events. And as such, people go to extreme lengths to avoid them, procrastinating doing them for days, weeks, or even months—even though we know they're best for us and our companies.

This is due to the fact that underlying our worst procrastination is a deep underlying fear that doesn't go away. Maybe it's a fear of failure . . . or fear of success. Maybe it's a fear of being vulnerable or hurting someone else's feelings.

But there's always a fear behind it and that's why we procrastinate. Procrastination is always rooted in some form of fear.

But where does this fear come from?

Best-selling author Mark Manson decided to address this issue and created "Manson's Law of Avoidance," which states that the more something threatens your identity, the more you will avoid doing it. (Manson's Law is basically just a particular encapsulation of self-verification theory from social psychology.)

That means that the more something threatens to change how you view yourself and how you believe yourself to be, the more you will procrastinate about ever getting around to doing it. If you believe, for example, that you are a good boss and that employees like good bosses, it's very difficult to fire people. You avoid that conflict like the plague.

The crazy thing about Manson's Law is that it can apply to both good and bad things in one's life. As a CEO, increasing revenue can threaten your identity just as much as losing all your money.

Generally, the hardest things for us to do in life are full of emotional resistance. Whether it's finally moving away from our hometown for a better job or shutting up and starting the new business that we're always telling people about, we avoid these things because, in some way, they threaten to contradict the beliefs we have about ourselves. The employee doesn't leave his job because he secretly believes he's not good enough to be successful anywhere else. The executive never sits down with her boss to talk about a pay raise because, ironically, the possibility of failure would threaten her belief that she's smart and capable of anything.

The belief always takes precedence. Until we change how we view ourselves—what we believe we are and what we are not—we cannot adopt the decisions and behaviors we spend so much time avoiding.

The solution is to change your mind-set and change your life. Lose the image of who you are. Psychologically speaking, your idea of who "you" are is constructed throughout your life with a bunch of random experiences. When we let go of the stories we tell about ourselves, to ourselves, we free ourselves up to take action (and fail) and grow.

When the boss admits to herself, "You know, maybe I'm not a great leader or good at managing people," then she is suddenly free to act and terminate the toxic employee. She has no identity to protect.

When the salesperson admits to themself, "You know, maybe I'm not above prospecting, maybe I'm just scared," then they are free to be ambitious again and have no reason to feel threatened.

Manson's recommendation: redefine yourself in mundane and broad ways. Choose to see yourself not as this corporate star or undiscovered genius. Choose to see yourself not as some horrible victim or dismal failure. Instead, see yourself as just a few simple things: a boss, a spouse, a parent, a friend.

This often means giving up some idealistic and flowery ideas about yourself. That you're uniquely intelligent, or spectacularly talented, or stunningly attractive, or especially victimized in ways other people simply could never relate to.

We like telling ourselves these stories. They make us feel good. But they also hold us back.

Define yourself in the simplest, most mundane, and broadest ways possible. Because the narrower and rarer the identity you choose for yourself, the more everything will begin to threaten you. And with those threats will come the avoidance, the fear, and the procrastination of all the things that really matter.

Never Lose. Win Or Learn.

Nelson Mandela said it best when he told the world, "I never lose. I either win or learn."

The best coaches in the world create game plans based on the approach of setting intentions over expectations. In the National Football League, for example, coaches map out the first drive down the field but include alternate plays depending on the exact situation the team faces.

Even the most detailed game plans are based on intentions, not expectations. That's why we hear the best coaches in the NFL, such as Bill Belichick of the New England Patriots, tout their approach to game planning as preparing their teams for "situational football." It puts players in a position to adjust on every play, to learn from plays that don't work, and to do better the following play.

The greatest coaches are the ones whose plans are intention-based because they and their teams can pivot in real time. If they walked into the locker room with a very fixed mind-set of "My expectation is we're going to win the game by doing this," they wouldn't be in the league for too long.

Let's consider a football game where one team has let up a lot of rushing yards. The other team might plan to run the ball a lot to take advantage of their opponent's weakness. If it works, that's great. You win.

But what if it doesn't work? You might continue to run and run and run, expecting it to work eventually. But what if the other team anticipated your game plan and adjusted their approach? If you don't pivot, you lose.

A better approach would be to enter the game with an intention to run but the flexibility to adjust if you learn that it's not working. Then, you'd adjust much quicker to a passing approach or play-action when you realized your running game wasn't moving the ball that day.

In business, we go into each day like coaches go into each game. We make the best plan possible based on the information we have available to us. Then, when things don't go according to plan, the best entrepreneurs adjust. Call it "situational leadership."

When things go well, we win. When they don't, the best leaders learn and pivot.

The Only Way To The Summit

Recently, I was struck by an essay by climber Ben Rueck, who wrote about the pressure of expectations for a Salt Lake Climbing Festival's "Art of the Project" series.[33]

"As kids we'd embrace perceived failures by crying, throwing a tantrum, and then moving onto the next adventure or random life encounter without a second thought," writes Rueck.

So what happened in that time from being a child to adulthood? When did we become afraid to make mistakes? When did we stop experiencing the unknown? When did we stop exploring the world around us with curiosity? One word—expectations.[34]

As Rueck continues, he describes how expectations we have of ourselves and others create "insane" barriers.

> Many people have unreasonable levels of expectation that rarely reflect reality . . .. Expectations have a nasty habit of ruining life experiences and creating a fantasy world in which people have preconceived notions. When we give into those, the world becomes a lot less interesting.[35]

Rueck challenges readers to replace expectation with intention, "a fluid concept that allows us to adapt to events quickly and efficiently."[36] In Rueck's world of rock climbing, setting intentions versus expectations is often a matter of life or death as he navigates up the side of a mountain.

"I started having a set of intentions prior to attempting my project," he writes.

> That way when I was climbing and didn't reach my first intention, I could reevaluate my particular set of circumstances and make adjustments to learn without going through all the negative cycles and mental barriers . . . As we grow in experience, no matter how

much work you put into something, the reality is: It's never what you expect.[37]

When Rueck reaches each summit, we can be sure of a few things. Most relevant to this discussion, we know that his climb likely didn't go according to plan. The precise path he took was not likely the one he envisioned when looking up from the bottom. But he achieved his intention of reaching the summit by making a series of pivots along the way.

We might not face a literal free fall in our worlds when things don't go according to plan, but we can learn a lot from Rueck's example. We will never reach our own summit if we set expectations and refuse to adjust. The only way to the top is through setting intentions.

Your Child, The Doctor

One of the most common examples of the problem with setting expectations versus setting intentions involves a parent's vision for their child's future. If you've ever spoken with parents expecting their first child, you've likely been on the receiving end of a long list of hopes and dreams. But what if you fast forward twenty or thirty years? How many times do you think the child's life turned out exactly as the parents had planned? The answer is pretty much never.

Yet every parent wants the best for their child. Often it sounds something like this: "I want my child to grow up to be a contributing member of society, have high self-esteem, be successful, and be happy."

Some parents take it a step further, though. In those cases, they might say, "Our child is going to be a doctor." Many of those parents take things another step forward and push their kids toward the life that the parents wanted for their child, instead of what their child ends up wanting. They expect their child to pursue a certain path. They define success for their child based on *their* view of what's best for their child. And if their child becomes an accountant or restaurant manager instead of a doctor, some parents consider that a failure—even if their child is happy. They expected their child to become a doctor. When the child doesn't comply, they and the child are considered failures.

But what if we change only one fact from this example? What if, instead of them setting the expectation that their child would become a doctor, the parents set the following intention: "We will help our child become fulfilled and financially independent by pursuing a career that matches their talents and passions."

This shift changes everything. The parents who wished for their child to become a doctor likely did so with good intentions. They wanted the child to become respected and financially successful. But what if they just set an intention of helping their child achieve fulfillment and success instead of adding the expectation of them doing so as a doctor? The answer is that both the child and the parents would likely end up better off.

I'll use an early example from my parenting as another example of how this happens with families. I'm a baseball player (yes, I *still* play at over fifty years old). I could have "decided" that my son would play baseball growing up. Thankfully, I avoided falling into that trap because it was also very clear to me very early on that my son had no interest in the sport. So, instead of force-feeding him the sport and having him resent me, I supported him as he pursued what made *him* happy.

I said to him, "I really want you to be healthy. I want you to have good self-esteem." And I let him pick the sports he played, which ended up being football and wrestling. Now that he's nearly a 30-year-old man, he thanked me for doing so because he learned several valuable life lessons from those sports.

Had I set the *expectation* of him playing baseball, he would have missed out on those lessons. Instead, I pivoted my intentions for him to be healthy and happy, and he flourished.

Intentions And Impact

As leaders in business, we might not be investing in start-up entrepreneurs, but we're investing in the future of our businesses. We might not be putting together game plans, but we *are* putting together business plans. And we might not be climbing mountains, pushing team members toward baseball or medical school, but we *are* leading our team members and ourselves toward a bigger vision of success and fulfillment.

To succeed in achieving what really matters in business is to do so by setting intentions, not expectations. It is the key to being flexible, resourceful, and focused on what really matters.

With that in place, you're ready to learn the simple four-part process you can use to guide you forward to diagnose and redirect when your mindset becomes unhealthy, your leadership loses its focus on ATV, or your intentions morph into expectations. We'll do that next.

Insights
- Intentions are adaptive, expectations are fixed.
- Never lose. Either win or learn.
- Situational leadership is more productive than expectational leadership.
- COVID-19 is a great example of a time when we can look for opportunity within a tragedy.

Questions For Reflection
- Where in your life (business, marriage, parenting, etc.) can you pivot away from expectations and into intentions? (Make a list.)

Action Steps
- Seek to replace expectations with intentions in all aspects of life.
- Learn to pivot quickly on the playing field of life—away from what is not working—and seek alternative routes up your mountain. The journey is never what you expect.
- Reflect on your childhood. What did you learn from your family regarding expectations?
- Reflect on what you are teaching your children regarding expectations. What would you like to change about your parenting around this?

Additional Resources
Visit ExtraordinaryAdvisors.com for more exclusive coaching tips.

Chapter 4

The E-4 Process That Can Improve Your Mind-Set, Leadership, And Results

"Learning is more effective when it is an active rather than a passive process."
—*Kurt Lewin, Change Management & Group Dynamics Thinker/Psychologist*

If I could give you one simple formula to help you navigate the ups and downs of entrepreneurship, it would be the E-4 Process I share with you in this chapter (which I call the E-4 Process because it gives you four steps to becoming extraordinary in any situation). This is the exact process I use to help my clients navigate pretty much everything they face in their business and personal lives. Its roots are in the active learning cycle methodology.

The secret to its impact is in its flexibility. It can help you with your mind-set, your leadership, your intention setting, and more. That's because it incorporates mind-set, leadership, and intention setting into the four simple steps. It's a holistic process designed to get our mind-set, leadership, and intentions aligned. Even better, it's simple. In fact, the four steps are so simple that it almost feels anticlimactic to share them. But the simplicity is what makes the steps so powerful. Anyone can use them to achieve a better future. The E-4 Process is a loop that never ends—as new insights are gained, they can be dropped into the iterative loop.

Over time, it will become instinctual for you to shift into walking through these four steps anytime you feel out of alignment. You'll feel a twinge in your stomach and know that you're heading in the wrong direction. That's your body telling you to pause and pivot. And these are the four steps to doing so.

Four Steps To A Successful Future

No matter where you go or what you do, the first step toward meaningful change is to recognize your problem. Only then can you make the right shift. When I was $600,000 in debt, I needed to figure out exactly what got me there before I could fix the problem. Of course, Greg and I discovered many problems, which is to be expected when things get that bad. But the big problem we discovered, business-wise, was my margins. My margins were so thin that I had zero room for error. Only by recognizing that could I shift toward a better, more secure future.

No matter what you face moving forward, here are your four steps to a more successful future:

1. Identify what's not working.
2. Set a new intention.
3. Plan and take action.
4. Get help, iterate, pivot as necessary, and repeat.

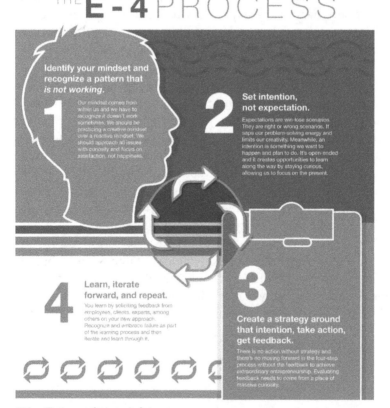

THE **E-4** PROCESS

1 Identify your mindset and recognize a pattern that *is not working.*

Our mindset comes from within us and we have to recognize it doesn't work sometimes. We should be practicing a creative mindset over a reactive mindset. We should approach all issues with curiosity and focus on satisfaction, not happiness.

2 Set intention, not expectation.

Expectations are win-lose scenarios. They are right or wrong scenarios. It saps our problem-solving energy and limits our creativity. Meanwhile, an intention is something we want to happen and plan to do. It's open-ended and it creates opportunities to learn along the way by staying curious, allowing us to focus on the present.

4 Learn, iterate forward, and repeat.

You learn by soliciting feedback from employees, clients, experts, among others on your new approach. Recognize and embrace failure as part of the learning process and then iterate and learn through it.

3 Create a strategy around that intention, take action, get feedback.

There is no action without strategy and there's no moving forward in the four-step process without the feedback to achieve extraordinary entrepreneurship. Evaluating feedback needs to come from a place of massive curiosity.

Yes, it's that simple. If all you take with you from this book are these four steps, your future will be bright. For the rest of this chapter, I'll walk you through these four steps using examples from mind-set, leadership, and intention setting to show you how flexible yet effective these steps are.

Using The Four Steps To Maintain A Creative Mind-Set

In Chapter 1, we addressed the importance of a creative, not reactive, mind-set. This can be a challenge, however. Even the most creative-minded leader will end up reactive from time to time. For this example, let's use the example of someone asking us for a discount we don't want to give. Here's how the four steps would help.

1. Identify What's Not Working

We're on the phone with a potential client who asks for a discount or special terms. What do you do? Many leaders will get hijacked. They will feel their blood pressure rise. They'll start feeling confrontational or acting defensive.

Our awareness that we are having those feelings are your hint that you're heading toward reactive thinking. If you pause and enter the E-4 Process before responding, you will recognize what's happening in your mind.

We get heightened by those types of requests. We think it's ridiculous. People wouldn't go into a fancy steak house and ask for a discount just because Applebee's sells top sirloin for half the price. But so many people feel almost entitled to demand a discount in other business situations.

If you don't pause, your reaction might be to immediately blast the person for requesting preferential treatment. Or your Imposter Syndrome will take over and convince you to give the discount, because "everyone else is doing it." Instead, I want you to pause and recognize what's happening inside you. Then move onto step two.

2. Set a New Intention

The next step in the process is to set a new intention. Our intention for the call might be to simply close the client for our standard terms. Their request at least temporarily puts that into doubt. So what's a new intention that works for you? That might be to identify whether the client is worth salvaging in a way that defends what's most important to you.

When we do that, we would recognize that it's normal for things to not go as planned. But shifting toward a new intention helps us choose to not let the situation take over our emotions and to reflect on what's truly important to us.

We know not everything goes according to plan. If it did, I wouldn't have been $600,000 in debt, and you likely wouldn't be reading this book. But I was, and you are, and that's because things go wrong all the time, and the people who invest in personal and professional growth will end up better off than those who don't.

Here we would recognize that it's normal for someone to ask for a discount. It happens all the time. There are literally buyers who go to classes to learn how to beat up vendors for price discounts, and it's a badge of honor for them to wear when they get one. They're trained that way. So, as entrepreneurs, we have to know that people are going to ask us for discounts. And we have to recognize that we're going to get reactive and emotional when that happens.

Choose not to get heightened by the request. Instead, pause and realize that whatever is happening in the moment is likely very normal and identify what is truly important to us. In this case, it might be important to defend our price, but we might not care about other terms that would give a small win to the potential customer. Maybe we can give them better speed or quality, even if we can't give a discount.

3. Plan and Take Action

In this situation, we know our mind-set is the problem. But we're on the phone, so our ability to get outside help is limited. We could schedule a call later to give us time to get help. But at this point in the conversation, we don't know enough about the request, so we would enter into learning mode to be able to navigate next steps. In this case, the best approach is to use curiosity.

Continuing our example, instead of offering better speed or quality and trying to find middle ground, I would approach the request with massive curiosity and ask questions to see what is really going on with the person. I'd say, "I understand that you are asking for a discount. Why is that important to you?"

If they say, "I never pay retail," or something like that, I would double down on massive curiosity and ask clarifying questions. Often, a real reason arises that helps me offer something while maintaining what's important to me without having to reschedule the call.

With pricing, I might say, "It would not be fair to give you one price that I wouldn't give someone else, so help me better understand how I can give you a discount when it goes against our core value of integrity? I want to be of service to you [which anchors me into being creative] but I need to keep to my core value of integrity and honor the customers who have paid our rates for years. Help me better understand your request."

They will often respond to say they understand and continue the conversation to find some other middle ground that makes both of us happy. If not, I will, which leads us to the final step of shifting from a reactive mind-set to a creative mind-set. If I don't recognize an immediate solution but want to salvage the relationship, I'll reschedule the call to move onto the next step: get help, iterate, and pivot toward finding a final resolution one way or another.

4. Get Help, Iterate, Pivot as Necessary, and Repeat
By the time we get to step four, we have shifted away from a reactive mind-set. Now we need to get help and stay in a creative mind-set to find a solution that works for both parties. If we can find one in the moment, great. If not, we iterate a few times, pivot as necessary, and repeat the process until we know whether we need to move on or reschedule the call.

With the discount example, I could reach out to a coach or my team to get input as I continue to work through what's truly important to find the middle ground. By now, the person on the other line is likely a bit tired and open to giving you the bottom line about what's truly important to them. If

I can get that information from them, I can connect with the right people to help me offer something of value to them while maintaining what's important to me.

And if the discount example sounds a little *too* vivid to be *just* a hypothetical, it's because it's not. It happened all the time to me in my business. At first, I'd move straight into reactive thinking. Once I was able to shift into creative mode, everything improved. I was surprised at how easy it was to get what I needed while maintaining a creative mind-set. I was also surprised by the reasons people offered for wanting a discount once I moved through the four steps. I learned that for many companies, trying their buyers and asking for discounts is part of their culture. I'd rarely need to reschedule the call to get help. Almost every time, the process helped me find a solution or realize it wasn't going to work out.

One time, the guy on the line was pretty aggressive. He kept asking for a discount even after I told him I couldn't offer him one. Finally, I asked him why he kept asking. That's when he told me his boss required him to aggressively ask for discounts. I understood where he was coming from, so I offered to tell his boss that he beat me up for a while, we were one minute from walking away, and he got the best possible deal. He agreed and we sealed the deal on my terms.

In this case, we made a deal that got him what he wanted without having to give up a thing, all because I stayed in a creative mind-set.

If you struggle with this, I encourage you to give yourself some grace and practice self-compassion. No matter how much we work on improving our mind-set, we will all fall into periods of time when we need extra help. While a lot of that help can come from having a coach on call to guide us or a group available for accountability or support, you're the only one who can take action. That's why I created this simple E-4 Process you can use on a daily basis to help you identify and self-correct when you're heading in the wrong direction from a mind-set perspective.

In 2014, I hired a new coach, Dr. Daniel Friedland, CEO of SuperSmartHealth and the author of *Leading Well from Within: A Neuroscience and Mindfulness-Based Framework for Conscious Leadership.*

I still worked with Greg, and continue to do so informally, but I'm a big believer in the value of having a team of advisers. Dr. Friedland, who is still my coach as I write this book, also focuses on different pieces of entrepreneurship than Greg.

One of my most valuable takeaways I have experienced from working with Dr. Friedland was developing this E-4 Process. I had benefited from mind-set work for many years, and Daniel encouraged me to simplify it into a simple process. After I did, my mind-set work became much easier and more effective. I have since used it to help many of my clients do the same. The bottom line is, when we can train ourselves to shift from reactive thinking to creative thinking, we will be in a much better position to improve. We won't let ourselves fall into a trap of naked positive thinking because we take action and iterate as we go. We won't hold ourselves back by setting expectations. We won't let a fear of vulnerability keep us from leading well. We'll recognize our current situations and use the analytics and support systems we have around us to move forward. We'll avoid falling deep into a world of suck and instead send ourselves on a path forward toward success.

The best part about it is that we can achieve all of that, and more, by following this simple E-4 Process.

Using The Four Steps To Help Maintain ATV Leadership

If we know how important it is to maintain ATV leadership, why do so many of us slip into less healthy and productive leadership styles? Easy. We're human. If we were perfect, you wouldn't need this book and I wouldn't be writing it. But we're not. We're all far from perfect. And the E-4 Process can help us catch ourselves and pivot when we slip away from leading our teams—and ourselves—well.

In Chapter 2, I mentioned how my business and I benefitted by following Jack Stack's suggestion to lead with financial transparency and open-book management. Like I mentioned, posting all our financial numbers for team members wasn't easy to do, but it helped everyone make better decisions in real-time.

For this example, we'll use the E-4 Process in the context of a hypothetical leader. Let's assume the leader is on the phone with me. They were struggling to motivate their team members and hired me to help them become a better leader. After several minutes, I get a sense that they've been leading like I had been, by being inauthentic, hiding embarrassing information from team members, and pretending to have all the answers. I encourage them to spend the next thirty days focusing on ATV. As part of that, we determine that open-book management is a good idea.

The leader understands why it could be helpful but wants to avoid implementing it out of fear that it will negatively impact performance. But they know it's been helpful in many organizations. Here's how the E-4 Process could help.

1. Identify What's Not Working
The leader has spent years keeping the full picture of company performance close to the vest. He shares only high-level information with team members but without context, so the information isn't very helpful. He does not teach his team basic business financial literacy. Our plan involves doing exactly what I did with Diversified Industrial Staffing and posting all financial numbers on a weekly basis. He has the printouts ready and has scheduled a meeting to discuss performance with his team.

When the day comes, he has two choices: he can move forward as planned or cancel the meeting. That morning, his stomach is in knots. He doesn't want to reveal the extent of the problems. He fears his team will lose confidence in him. His Imposter Syndrome is flaring like a California wildfire. So what does he do? If he's been working with me, he knows that the pain in his gut is a signal that he's falling out of alignment, so he pauses and shifts to the four-part process.

In this case, he reminds himself that as scary as this is, keeping the numbers close to the vest wasn't working. He starts thinking more objectively and likely hears my voice reminding him that the best leaders are those who lead through ATV. He's still not comfortable, but he recognizes what's not working.

2. Set a New Intention

Next, he shifts to setting a new intention for the day. In this case, his feeling of fear likely means he is in danger of falling back into setting expectations and not intentions. He is pondering leaning away from, not into, this uncomfortable conversation with his team. Like the NFL team refusing to stop running the ball when it wasn't working, he realizes he needs to stop hiding the numbers because it isn't working. Instead, he needs to pivot to setting a new intention.

In this case, his intention in sharing the numbers is to give full context to his team so they can better perform, and so he can lead with more transparency moving forward. He's now thinking more objectively and creatively.

3. Plan and Take Action

With his intention set, he might put together a plan based on his intention. He decides what numbers are important to share. He decides how often he will share numbers. And he decides how he will present the numbers to his team. Once his plan is in place, he would schedule the meeting and present his plan to his team.

4. Get Help, Iterate, Pivot as Necessary, and Repeat

The fourth step in this hypothetical could occur before or after the meeting. Before the meeting, he might call me and run through his plan to get feedback and practice presenting it. After the meeting, he might reach out to me to get help based on the feedback he receives from presenting the information to his team. Like most initiatives, the leader recognizes that things never go exactly according to plan. Thus, he prepares himself for questions, adjustments, and revisiting the four steps in the future.

By pausing and moving through the four steps, the leader is able to avoid several negative results, including reactive thinking (canceling the meeting), ditching ATV leadership (hiding the numbers), and setting expectations (the old way of closed-book management would suddenly start working).

Using The Four Steps To Set Intentions, Not Expectations

Barbara Corcoran's experiment with VHS-tape real estate tours is not only a good example of setting intentions rather than expectations but it is also a perfect example of how the E-4 Process can help us avoid shifting back into expectation thinking.

Specifically, when VHS tapes proved too slow to work, Corcoran didn't quit. She didn't let her intention about video tours revolutionizing real estate sales turn into expectations and keep trying to use VHS tapes. She pivoted toward using the internet to achieve the same result in a different way. Years later, what began as a desire to reduce the time it took to tour real estate turned from an expensive disaster into a multi-million-dollar success story.

1. Identify What's Not Working

Before her VHS experiment, Corcoran saw that the traditional way of in-person tours was not working. High-end shoppers value their time very highly as do people moving from out of town.

2. Set a New Intention

Corcoran set an intention to use video tours as a way to reduce the time it took to conduct a real estate search. Video could enable her clients to narrow down the list of properties they needed to view in person. She could also open up New York City apartments to a wider audience by making it easier for people around the world to tour apartments using video.

3. Plan and Take Action

Corcoran and her team decided to send VHS tapes to potential clients. She put together the plan and sent out the tapes.

As discussed before, however, this was far from perfect, and the real estate listings on the VHS tapes were often obsolete by the time they arrived. Corcoran needed a different way to achieve her intention.

4. Get Help, Iterate, Pivot as Necessary, and Repeat

After taking action, Corcoran quickly learned from clients, employees, and Wall Street experts that VHS tapes moved too slowly. That's important. She didn't learn that her intention was inaccurate. High-end shoppers wanted a better way to shop for real estate. It was her plan that was flawed. So she took the advice and direction from clients, employees, and Wall Street experts and iterated, pivoting from VHS tapes to the internet.

Corcoran's new plan of using the internet was a big success. Anyone around the world could access her listings in a heartbeat. In the end, her pivot from VHS tapes to the internet birthed a multi-million-dollar real estate venture.

Start Simple

Author John Gall said it best in his book, *Systemantics: How Systems Work and Especially How They Fail*:

> A complex system that works is invariably found to have evolved from a simple system that worked. A complex system designed from scratch never works and cannot be patched up to make it work. You have to start over with a working simple system.[38]

That's really the key to using the E-4 Process in your business and personal life. Keep it simple. Just ask yourself one question when you feel yourself get out of alignment: What's not working? When you identify that, set a new intention (and don't have an expectation). Then get help, plan, and pivot. Iterate and repeat as necessary. Be deliberate at first. It will feel awkward to pause and ask yourself those questions. In my case, I ask my coaching clients these questions over and over again. It truly is the best and easiest way to keep from landing in a world of suck and redirect toward success.

Over time, it becomes second nature, and your natural instinct will be to pause, identify what's not working, set a new intention, get help, plan, and pivot, and then iterate and repeat. You'll be able to do it with even complex challenges. It will be your secret weapon. And it will all have evolved from four simple steps.

Insights

- Everyone gets triggered or becomes heightened. No one is immune to becoming reactive.
- Approach issues with massive curiosity instead of assumptions. Ask why-based questions numerous times to get to the core issue.
- Focus on your purpose or *why* to get unstuck with things that don't work.

Questions For Reflection

- Are there issues or topics that repeatedly cause me to become reactive? Look for patterns.
- What difficult conversations or decisions am I avoiding making? Why?
- Have we written down and shared our company core values with all team members? When faced with tough decisions, lean on your core values for guidance.

Action Steps

- To slow down our reactivity, we must first recognize that we are becoming triggered or reactive. The sooner we recognize this, the sooner we get to a creative mind-set.
- Lean into, not away from, difficult conversations.
- Have a trusted advisor, coach, or mentor to call when you can't self-manage your reactive mind-set.

Additional Resources

Friedland, Daniel. *Leading Well from Within: A Neuroscience and Mindfulness-Based Framework for Conscious Leadership.* San Diego: SuperSmartHealth, 2016.

Gall, John. *Systemantics: How Systems Work and Especially How They Fail.* New York: Quadrangle, 1977.

Also visit ExtraordinaryAdvisors.com to download a graphic representation of the E-4 Process plus additional exclusive coaching tips.

Part 2:
Taking Action

Chapter 5

Looping Toward Success

"Success is stumbling from failure to failure with no lack of enthusiasm."
— *Winston Churchill*

In the first part of the book, we worked through the three biggest challenges entrepreneurs face when it comes to themselves: mind-set, leadership, and being held back by expectations. We then saw how my simple E-4 Process can keep you from heading toward a world of suck and redirect you toward success no matter what challenge you face.

Over the rest of the book, we'll walk through the biggest challenges entrepreneurs face in their businesses. Having pulled myself up from the brink of disaster and then worked with hundreds of entrepreneurs, I've had a bird's eye view of countless problems that come up repeatedly in businesses.

In this chapter, I'll walk you through what I call looping toward success in business so you can prepare your business for the inevitable difficult times ahead. This is different from preparing ourselves as leaders and entrepreneurs, which we addressed in the first part. This is how we empower our team members to be more resilient and our businesses to be stronger.

Preparing our businesses and team members to navigate the ups and downs of business can be revolutionary for us as entrepreneurs. We will no longer have to do everything ourselves. We will be able to take vacations. We'll be able to delegate confidently and trust that we've built a real business that doesn't need us to do everything. We can breathe.

There's no denying, however, that there's no straight line to success. Entrepreneurs learn this pretty quickly. It reminds me of a meme I saw circulating about the year 2020, which I've recreated below.

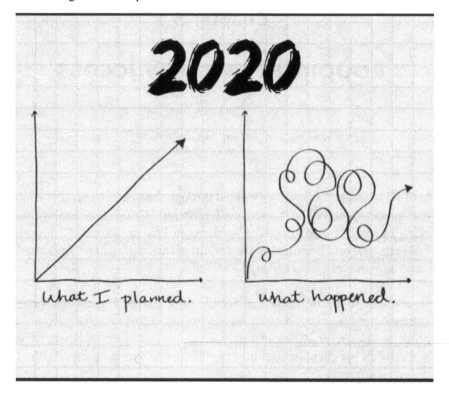

You can replace "2020" with "entrepreneurship" without changing a single other element. That's entrepreneurship. It's not linear. There's no straight line to success. There's just one, messy looping line. Even the best entrepreneurs' lines loop around, go up and down, backtrack and move forward. If their lines generally loop up and to the right over the long term, they achieve success. If not, everything will suck.

History is full of leaders, explorers, coaches, and others who've followed this looping line of success, experiencing multiple dips, twists, and turns along the way. Of course, we might describe those dips, twists, and turns as failures. But if you keep on going, and keep working the E-4 Process, you can pivot.

As far back as the 1400s, when Christopher Columbus set out to reach Asia, leaders "failed" their way to success. In Columbus's case, he stumbled on the Americas. And consider the thousands of people who've set out to summit Mount Everest, only to turn back around and then up again once they have figured out how to acclimate to the dangerous conditions. Not a single human who achieved high levels of success has successfully avoided the dreaded loop. We all loop around. And we all fall back on the E-4 Process many times throughout our lives to avoid the suck and find sustained successes.

In this chapter, we'll learn more about the looping line toward success. We'll also learn how to prepare ourselves and our businesses to ensure that when we loop, we go upwards over the long term, even if we stumble in the short term.

As you might imagine, as with our mind-set, leadership, and intentions, we need to be flexible and intentional for it to work. We have to adjust and change. And we need to be committed to continually iterating and helping our teams do the same.

Before we do, we must first acknowledge an untold truth about entrepreneurship: when things suck in business, they suck more for the entrepreneur than anyone else. That's because when money gets distributed in business, entrepreneurs get paid last. Many early-stage entrepreneurs don't realize the sequence goes like this:

1.   Employees get paid first.
2.   Government gets paid second.
3.   Vendors get paid third.
4.   You, as the entrepreneur, get paid fourth—if there's any money left.

When the success line loops, the first person to get paid is not you. That's why this chapter is so important. You need to build your business so even the loopiest of loops don't take you out. You will never avoid the loops, but you can build your business so it can survive them.

That's a looping line of success. You want to build a business. But we need to look at what a journey from suck to success looks like. We also need to look at where entrepreneurs most frequently falter in such a way that it can take down their entire organization. These common struggles include not branding ourselves, giving away our services for free, and refusing to embrace small failures. Importantly, they also include failing to create a culture of trust and making revenue, not the more important margins, the key metric that demonstrates the health of a company.

Before we look at this journey, let's use an example from my business to demonstrate the looping line of success.

The Loop Heard 'Round The World

Like many businesses, my coaching business—Extraordinary Advisors—followed the looping line of success during the COVID-19 pandemic of 2020. Leading into 2020, my business and margins were strong. I was helping a lot of entrepreneurs as a keynote speaker and coach. When I first pursued becoming a public keynote speaker, my goal was to place myself in front of my ideal audience—entrepreneurs and other business leaders who might hear something from the stage that would resonate with them.

The idea was for them to then hire me to coach them, their teams, or their businesses. I even hired my own speaking coach, who advised me to get on as many stages as possible—anything from a free local speech in metro Detroit to a regional or national keynote speech.

By January 2020, I was positioned to really start making an impact. I had multiple speeches scheduled for the months ahead. And then COVID-19 hit—everything got canceled, changed, or delayed until 2021. I'd be lying if I didn't admit that it hurt. But, like we talked about when we discussed the Stockdale Paradox, my brutal reality became that I could no longer physically speak from the stage. It was just not an option. The platform was no longer available to me.

Since I no longer had that pipeline of opportunities to attract coaching clients, I chose to pivot. I had to deal with my brutal reality: *I can't speak from the stage right now. But I will get through this and I will lean into the uncomfortable moments.*

So how would I reinvent my business? How could I continue my why of improving lives?

Instead of letting failure get the best of me, I made the best of it. I went back to my E-4 Process, first recognizing what wasn't working for me—speaking in person from the stage. Then I followed the second step, setting an intention, not an expectation. My intention: *How can I still get my message out to the world? How can I be of service to others if I can't do it from the stage? How else could I reach out to business leaders? How else could I reach out to communities? How else could I reach out the world to deliver my message?*

I got help from trusted advisers, planned, and pivoted. I realized I could reach out to the organizers of the canceled speeches and offer webinars or conversations with their members to still be of service to them. They'd already booked my time and prepaid me to appear, so I wanted to make sure I was giving them something of value in return. And I kept iterating and repeating the process to achieve my intention.

Within months, my schedule filled, and I was able to achieve my intention and even attract coaching clients during a time when many other coaches were hemorrhaging business.

I also went to Facebook and LinkedIn and offered free 30-minute coaching sessions for entrepreneurs and CEOs on how to handle chaos and uncertainty. I sent text messages reaching out to other possible clients—offering everything for free. I felt uncomfortable asking for business during such a crisis, so I decided to just be a resource for them. My outreach was about servant leadership, not selling services.

I was constantly reminded that my speaking gigs were lost, so it was scary for me to be doing so much for free. By leaning into the uncomfortable, I was able to get over it. Suddenly, I was speaking with forty-two entrepreneurs from around the world within a six-week period. Soon, I was back on an upward trajectory again and even better prepared for some of those dips and twists I'll inevitably face in the future. And I was living my *why*. I improved the lives of many of the entrepreneurs I spoke with, garnering several Facebook testimonials and recommendations.

So let's take a closer look at the looping line of success in your world and how you can strengthen your business so you can be better positioned for the future. We'll start with your brand. Because as I've learned with Extraordinary Advisors, forward momentum comes only when you have a firm idea of who you are and where you are going as a business. As I've learned, by having a clearly stated brand, you'll draw the ideal client to you. And that's really what it means to build a solid brand.

My COVID-19 Suck vs. Success Mind-Set

Stockdale Paradox Brutal Reality: I can no longer speak from stage. Intention: I can get my message out to the world.

Get Help, Plan, and Pivot: Reaching out to clients. Speaking with forty-two entrepreneurs from around the world within a six-week period.

Iterate and Repeat: Learned from what was working. Did more of that. Kept going.

Branding Yourself

When I work with entrepreneurs about building stronger, more successful businesses, one of the first concepts we work to improve is their branding. It might sound counterintuitive, but it's true. You and everyone around you needs to know who you are as an entrepreneur. That helps everyone make better decisions about you. The same is true for your business. When you, your team, and your customers know who you are as a business—and who you are not—it helps everyone make better decisions in your business. That's why it's so important to be intentional about branding yourself and your business.

So, if you want to get and stay on the right trajectory toward success for your business, don't do anything else until you have your business brand established. Your brand is your business's reputation. It calls attention to your business—the right attention, if you do it well. Similar to your "why" or *ikigai,* you may try several different "brands" for your business before you figure out who you are and who you aren't.

Importantly, clear branding helps avoid one of the biggest problems many entrepreneurs face: trying to be all things to all people. It's the solution to the problem because it lets everyone know who you are and who you aren't. "A lot of entrepreneurs are not intentional about the brand, or very rarely think about the brand, when they create a business," says brand expert Deb Gabor, author of *Brand Is Sex* and *Irrational Loyalty.* "And so many brands go to market being a great solution to a problem and having some kind of unique bell or whistle. But when you don't pay attention to creating a brand that creates an emotional bond with your customer, you're opening yourself up for competition."[39]

As Deb explains, your brand:
- Protects you from competitive threats,
- increases the financial viability and value of your business,
- allows you to scale more rapidly and more profitably, and
- provides a tangible financial benefit to the organization.[40]

"People's brains love and need stories," Deb says. "Your brand is a shortcut for the story of how you elevate your customers' self-concept. If ice cream brands marketed themselves on the basis of 'It's cold, and it's sweet, and it comes in three different sizes,' there wouldn't be Ben & Jerry's. There wouldn't be Hägen-Dazs. There wouldn't be as many people who buy ice cream. But when you have a very strong brand that creates a condition of irrational loyalty, it increases sustainability and profitability and contributes a tangible financial value to the overall valuation of the company."[41]

When I first started my business, I had built Diversified Industrial Staffing to be a generalized staffing agency. That meant I was being evaluated against real generalized staffing agencies. Unfortunately, generalized staffing agencies had razor-thin margins and, often, long payment cycles. While that worked for companies large enough to have deep pockets to take on loss-leader-type volume business, it nearly made me bankrupt. When I decided to rebrand my business to be a more niched staffing agency, I was able to break free from what my clients expected of a bigger agency and shift their expectations to those of a niched agency. I was able to do this because we focused on serving the candidate—not the client—first. The job candidate was the center of the increased demand/diminished supply equation. By focusing on the candidate piece of the employer/employee relationship dynamic, we were no longer a commodity staffing provider.

We had the candidate who was in demand. This allowed me to quickly raise my margins and shorten my receivable timelines.

This can be a big struggle for entrepreneurs who are so used to running around putting out fires all day—especially the ones who are also the chief arsonist in their business. Pausing to take a bigger-picture look at their business landscape and look at where they can own a market can feel like something they don't have time to do. And they're so stressed out that it's hard to even know what they want to do.

If that sounds like you, don't worry. First, you can always get help from someone who isn't so buried in the day-to-day as you are to help you look at your business with fresh eyes. Ask trusted friends or hire a coach to help.

You are on the frontlines, taking your hero's journey. A coach has a 10,000-foot view of your hero's journey and can advise you of rough patches you have not encountered yet. Second, always remember that the last step in the E-4 Process is to iterate and repeat. Everything we do is just our "current version" of whatever we're building. Maybe you're on version 1.0 of your business right now. Maybe you're on version 10.7. (Think of Microsoft software versions and the continual updates you receive.) It doesn't matter. What does matter is that you brand yourself and iterate moving forward. This is especially important with branding because the more specific you can be with branding, the easier it is for your ideal customer to work with you. Why? Because they know who you are, allowing you to become successful. So, if you're not sure what you want your branding to be, don't stress about being perfect today. Start more general and then work on getting more specific as you go.

A perfect example of starting as generalists and becoming more specific upon learning the market (a focusing exercise most entrepreneurs call niching) would be my nieces Sara and Lindsay. Like most entrepreneurs, they became more successful as they got more niched. They started out as a healthcare staffing company focused on providing physical therapists, occupational therapists, and speech therapists for hospitals and rehab facilities. Sara and Lindsay soon pivoted into public school settings—providing services to kids with autism—once they discovered the demand was high and that great behavioral healthcare providers were in short supply. Then they got extremely specific and further discovered a subcategory of registered behavioral technician (RBT) and board certified behavior analyst (BCBA) healthcare providers who were difficult to find with a strong growing demand.

Next, they decided to take a geographically targeted approach and went from serving twelve states in the western United States to just one: California. Sound counterintuitive? Sure, but it works. There is a saying that you can either go a mile wide and an inch deep or a mile deep and an inch wide. By narrowing their focus, Sara and Lindsay were able to scale almost immediately. They went a mile deep, and it paid off.

> Sometimes we think more is better. Most times, "more" simply dilutes the effort, and you miss the magic of leveraging once you decide on your path.

Once they became known as the go-to company in California, Sara and Lindsay had suitors lined up to buy their quickly growing healthcare business. After ten years of growth, Sara (37) and Lindsay (32) decided to sell their company in 2019 to a larger strategic competitor, the Stepping Stone Group. The combined company now stands as the single largest company of its type in the United States, with revenues approaching nearly a half a billion dollars.

My experience with branding myself continued long after I turned around Diversified Industrial Staffing. In fact, I might have had an even harder time branding my coaching business before I figured out who I was and who I wasn't. It took me two to three years to determine that my sweet spot was helping entrepreneurs and CEOs make the necessary (and frequently uncomfortable) changes to achieve their full business and personal potential. I made progress during those two to three years, but once I really branded myself, everything took off.

Find Your Niche . . . And Start Ugly

Strategy, action, and feedback go much smoother when you know exactly what you do best. Sure, you've started a dance studio franchise promising to revolutionize wellness around the world. But where can you be best-in-category? Go back to Chapter 1 and your *ikigai*. Maybe your strength is choreographing the music. Create a strategy around sharing dance soundtracks with the public. Or maybe it's appearing in the videos. Strategize how you can land speaking engagements. Record those speaking engagements or dance performances, post videos on YouTube, and gain followers who will eventually become clients. And if it's staying behind the scenes to work on the website, great. What matters is that you find your niche to help launch your own personal brand.

This may mean coming up with Version 6.0 of yourself, and that's OK. Just don't spend the next few months gripped by expectations. Take it from branding guru Chris Krimitsos, author of *Start Ugly: A Timeless Tale about Innovation & Change* and founder of Podfest Multimedia Expo: "It doesn't mean starting from scratch. It also means reinventing yourself. Because if you stay where you are, you're never going to be able to innovate with the times. Starting ugly is necessary to innovate. No matter where you're at as a parent, as a CEO, as a leadership coach, you need to start ugly now, and find what works next."[42]

How Your Brand Protects You During Turbulent Times

Your brand doesn't just help you get noticed in good times. In fact, it's probably more important for you during turbulent times, like the COVID-19 pandemic or the Great Recession of the late 2000s. As Deb Gabor and many other brand experts will tell you, how your brand shows up and acts when times are tough says more about you than what it does when times are good.

That applies on a macro- and micro-scale, too. On a micro-scale, if you have a company you're restarting, reigniting, and bringing back to market, start with your brand. "It's a demographic psychographic imperative today that you have a brand, because that is how people make decisions—95 percent of buying decisions happen outside of what's rational," says Gabor. "They happen in the heart. I sometimes talk to people who have great ideas. They're selling better mousetraps. And you can't sell mousetraps to people who don't have mice. You can't sell mousetraps to those who don't believe that mice are a problem. It's really hard to sell a better mousetrap if people don't have the why behind things. And your brand is the why."
Here are Gabor's tips on better branding:
- Aim your brand at a singular, ideal, archetypal customer. This is

not a demographic profile. It's not like, "We're for busy moms." I could sit in a room of 100 people who were all busy moms, and they would all differ based on the ages of their kids, what they do inside and outside the home, where they live, who they're married to. Are they married or not married? You can find an "avatar" by asking current customers or clients what they value about your business. Asking questions create patterns to help reveal the ideal client.

- Elevate your customers' self-concept through the use of their brand. Everybody lives their lives in accordance with Maslow's hierarchy of needs. At the most basic level, they need to take care of their physiological needs. At the highest level, they want to achieve self-actualization. Your brand is all about helping people navigate that hierarchy. If people associate getting closer to self-actualization by doing business with you, the stronger their bonds with you will become.

- Be singular. Figure out the one thing you offer that no one else can. The best brains in the world are not the ones that are simply "different." It's not enough to just be somewhat different than others. You have to be unique to truly stand out. Carve out your uniqueness. What is unique to you that no competitors can provide? By doing this, we draw in our ideal client. At the same time, we weed out clients who may not work so well with us. This can make entrepreneurs uncomfortable since they can't be all things to all people.

- Make your customer the hero in your world. In other words, your brand is about your customer, not you. If you go to your company's website and the first word is about you (such as highlighting your company name or the word "we"), you're doing it wrong. Talk directly to your ideal customer on your website.[44]

While branding yourself won't completely smooth out the loops on the looping line of success, it *will* make them smaller and provide forward momentum for your business. And without a specific brand, nobody will know who you are, what you can do for them, or how you'll help them rise up Maslow's hierarchy of needs.

Free Will

Are you giving away enough? For many entrepreneurs, the answer is no. This is a big problem in businesses and holds a lot of people back. Giving away more than you're comfortable doing is a huge strategy for success, especially for entrepreneurs looking to make an extraordinary impact.

As Jordan Steen explains on his Cereal Entrepreneur website, one of the greatest ways to generate authority and build trust with people is to give more than feels comfortable: "In order to build trust with your audience, you have to demonstrate authority and credibility by providing value. What better way to provide value than giving your prospective customers a glimpse of the value they'd be receiving by purchasing your product or service?"[45]

Now, I'm not suggesting that every entrepreneur reduce their prices to free or start tossing out new gizmos and gadgets as if they were throwing candy from a float in a Fourth of July parade. But for start-ups and businesses facing uncertain futures, being generous with your attention, time, and even certain services will pay off in the long run. As Steen continues, free offers contribute to ultimate success by:
- positioning you as an authority or expert,
- giving your audience a taste of what to expect when they work with you, and
- creating more opportunities for you to market your business.

In fact, Steen himself claims to have made $300,000 by giving away content. That seems like success to me.

Free Attention

Another great example of how generosity can lead to growth is how Gary Vaynerchuk has used free content to generate millions of dollars in revenue for multiple businesses.

Vaynerchuk is the author of several books himself and was featured as a success story in Joe Pulizzi's book, *Content, Inc.: How Entrepreneurs Use Content to Build Massive Audiences and Create Radically Successful Businesses.* This is a fascinating book about getting subscribers (or for entrepreneurs, customers) and then offering them tons of free content to nurture relationships with them to establish yourself in an industry.

Vaynerchuk grew his father's wine business from $3 million a year to $60 million a year in just five years by doing video wine tastings. He then launched VaynerMedia, a top social media consulting firm, to help other companies leverage attention. He now has a net worth of $160 million and nineteen million online fans. The secret to starting such a success? *Capturing attention.*

We can learn several lessons from Vaynerchuk's rise. Vaynerchuk's wine tastings gained attention for his refreshingly simple takes on wine. He wasn't the stuffy sommelier in a fancy restaurant. He was a regular guy talking about wine, something he knew a lot about. As Pulizzi writes in *Content, Inc.*, to prove your expertise, "[g]et focused on what makes you a leading expert in your field . . . Whether you are an entrepreneur in a start-up environment or running a Content, Inc. program in a large organization, you should always be thinking of how many ways you can monetize the asset of content you are constantly creating."[46]

Vaynerchuk gave away a lot of free content with his wine tastings, and nobody needed to buy the wine from his parents' store. They could have gone to their local store and looked for the same wines. But by being generous, many people did, and that's how he increased his parents' business from $3 million a year to $60 million so quickly. Today, Vaynerchuk frequently talks about the importance of attention. He emphasizes that we need attention before we sell anything, attention is an asset, and with vast attention comes great power.

Looping toward success can be so much easier if you leverage all the free attention you create through sharing generously with a well-defined audience. To start, ask yourself:
- Who is my ideal audience?
- What are their greatest pain points?
- What are people asking to buy?
- How do I get their attention?
- How do I deliver this?
- How do I monetize this?

Let's say I'm a fitness instructor hoping to sell a new line of hyperintelligent weights that instantly click together. My ideal audience would be fellow fitness instructors and those working out at home. Their greatest pain points would be struggling with outdated, awkward equipment. They're asking to buy something new to help them save time. I get their attention by establishing a strong social media presence—Facebook, Instagram, Twitter—and posting videos of superbuff people using the hyperintelligent weights while listening to the latest hip-hop tracks. I deliver by directing them to my website, where I give away water bottles for free. Then I monetize my idea by charging $400 for each set of weights I ship.

That's just one example of the new twist on the old marketing adage of spending a penny and getting a dollar. Here, you give away a penny and get millions of dollars.

Failure Is Not A Four-Letter Word

If you've homed in your brand and begun being generous with your ideal customers, you will be well on your way to building a stronger, more resilient business. That alone will set you apart from many entrepreneurs in the world. (I gave away my content during the COVID-19 pandemic by doing free 30-minute online coaching sessions and by appearing on webinars geared toward entrepreneurs wrapped up in their fear, self-doubt, and Itty Bitty Shitty Committees. I did all of this for free, and it netted me several coaching clients.)

Yet some entrepreneurs still carry with them an intense fear of failure. It doesn't matter if their brand is respected and their customers love them because of their generosity; their business is built upon an intense, and often irrational, fear of failure.

If you struggle to shake the fear of failure, it's really not your fault. The dictionary definition of failure is exactly what we try to avoid: the lack of success. But as we've discussed, Brian Scudamore and many others (including me) have achieved tremendous success with a history full of failures. In fact, the most successful people in the world aren't the ones who have avoided failure; they're the ones who have failed the most. Ask anyone you admire about his or her successes and failures. Chances are, their list of failures is much longer than their list of successes, but somehow, they still achieved great success. If that's the case, how can the definition of failure be lack of success?

"I give it my all and I learn. If I invested in the experience, and I learned from it, can I ever truly fail? Failures are nothing more than feedback along my path to success."—Dr. Daniel Friedland

It can't be. It's wrong. Failure isn't the lack of success, at least not in the long term. If anything, it's a stumble—or a loop—along a longer line to success. As we discussed in Chapter 3, when we talked about the concept of "win or learn," failure is really only possible if you give up. And even if you stumble, those stumbles don't start you back to the beginning of your journey. They just loop you around a few times. If you learn, iterate, and get back on the path of moving forward, each loop just makes you smarter and stronger. You win or you learn. And either way, you iterate and keep going.

Let's probe a little deeper into what failure is. A loop, a crooked line, a series of starts and stops or missteps. Envision it however you like. But failure is the story of almost all of our lives, a truth "Dilbert" creator Scott Adams explores in *How to Fail at Almost Everything and Still Win Big: Kind of the Story of My Life.* "Over the years I have cultivated a unique relationship with failure," he writes. "I invite it. I survive it. I appreciate it. And then I mug the shit out of it. Failure always brings something valuable with it. I don't let it leave until I extract that value. I have a long history of profiting from failure. My cartooning career, for example, is a direct result of failing to succeed in the corporate environment."[47]

His advice for looping toward success goes like this:
- Have a System, Not a Goal.
- Success Creates Passion More Than Passion Creates Success.
- Focus on Energy, Not Time.
- Fake It until You Make It.
- Increase Your Happy Thoughts Ratio.[48]

Unknowingly, I've been following these tips for years. When Diversified Industrial Staffing was about to go bankrupt, Greg (my brother and coach) and I came up with a system to move forward, not a concrete goal. We set out to improve margins and cash flow, knowing that would help solve pretty much all of my financial problems if I would continue to work on my mind-set, ATV leadership, and intention setting.

Because I learned those lessons the hard way, I was able to find greater success and fulfillment coaching entrepreneurs than I ever found with Diversified Industrial Staffing. I manage my clients and projects through energy—and yes, sometimes I've had to muster my creative mind-set. But I generally have more energy at the end of the day than I do at the beginning. As for increasing my happy thoughts outside of my business? Baseball, my family, and maple-smoked bacon will do that anytime. I also remind myself of my *why*: improve lives. I always go back to that core belief when I'm faced with tough client issues or challenges.

This concept of failure not being a four-letter word isn't a novel one, though. Walk through any bookstore and you'll find endless books about the new definition of failure. When I last googled "failing forward," I got nearly 900,000 results in 0.93 seconds. Business writers in *Forbes* and beyond have spent time questioning whether failure really leads to success for entrepreneurs, after all. But from my one-on-one work with leaders across dozens of industries, I've found that extraordinary entrepreneurship comes only from that looping string of failures.

Remember Barbara Corcoran? She rode a looping roller-coaster ride for years. Twenty jobs before opening the real estate office that she'd eventually sell for millions of dollars. If she'd stuck with her original job as a waitress, she might have experienced a straighter line to success. But that straight line might have led to her becoming a manager or owner someday. Instead, Corcoran corkscrewed her way to creating her own brand, building a multi-million-dollar business, and establishing a celebrity presence deciding the fate of future extraordinary entrepreneurs on *Shark Tank*.

Jacki Smith, founder and owner of Coventry Creations, is an example of an extraordinary entrepreneur who failed forward several times before finding success. (She is also a client of mine.) Jackie started a candle business in 1992 at age twenty-four with a $100 budget. In the business's first seven years, Jacki doubled her business every year.

"That was a crazy amount of growth for a twenty-four- to thirty-year old who didn't go to college and who was flying by the seat of her pants," says Smith, who got in her own way before getting slammed by outside turmoil. "From 2002 to 2008, it was a huge struggle. After 9/11 happened and the stock market crashed, I was not in control of my business."

A few bad experiences with people she hired to help her nearly bankrupted her along the way, too. So Jacki began reading, researching, and looking at everything from the inside out. That led to her discovering that her brand was much bigger than the candles she had been selling. Her customers wanted more from her, so she began expanding into oils, cards, books, and more. From that point forward, she kept true to the brand she wanted to build and tremendous success and fulfillment followed.

"I learned that it's OK if we don't want to grow to a multibillion dollar company, and it's OK if we don't want to grow to a $1 million company," she says. "We can be exactly what we want to be, because entrepreneurship is so personal."

Today, Jacki is one of the greatest examples of clients of mine who found success using the methods I share in this book. In doing so, she feels empowered by Coventry Creations and the path that led her there, as loopy as it was. "Without adversity, you will never grow," says Jacki, who even appreciates the adversity. "If you try to follow the straight line of nothing but success, then you've never really experienced the full potential."

Creating A Culture Of Trust

After branding yourself, building trust and attention through extraordinary generosity, and embracing the value of failure, you will begin to notice benefits far beyond making the loops less loopy for your business and building stronger bonds with customers. But those efforts typically focus your attention on connecting your business with your customers. You can build a decent business with just that foundation.

A foundation of strong connections with customers won't build you a strong enough foundation to build *extraordinary business*. To do that, you need to strengthen relationships among the people who help you run your business—you, your employees, your vendors, and your independent contractors.

You will benefit those relationships using the strategies from Part 1 and through branding, generosity, and embracing failure. But the bigger benefits for your business come from creating a culture of trust within the four walls of your organization. Way too many entrepreneurs skip this step, and it costs them dearly. They focus so much time and attention on external branding and marketing and not enough time on their team and company culture. We cannot forget our internal key stakeholders.

You must focus as much attention internally on your team and company culture as you do externally through branding and generosity. Otherwise, you're almost guaranteed to send yourself through a giant—and miserable— downward loop. It happens all the time. You have the best intentions but end up creating or tolerating a toxic culture that sends key team members running for cover. Eventually, your customers will learn that you and your company act one way internally and another with the outside world. When that happens, it won't be long before your looping line of success feels like a roller-coaster ride on a full stomach.

Fortunately, creating a culture of trust isn't complicated. But the impact of that culture is enormous. An *Inc.* magazine[49] article nicely summarizes the work of Paul J. Zak, author of *The Trust Factor: The Science of Creating High-Performance Companies*. Zak discovered that, compared with people at low-trust companies, people at high-trust companies report:
- 74 percent less stress,
- 106 percent more energy at work,
- 50 percent higher productivity,
- 13 percent fewer sick days,
- 76 percent more engagement,
- 29 percent more satisfaction with their lives, and
- 40 percent less burnout.[50]

"From 10 years of research," writes Inc.'s Melissa Levin, Zak "found that oxytocin levels significantly decrease when we feel stress. He also found a direct link between oxytocin levels and empathy, which is essential for creating trust-based relationships and trust-based organizations. The higher the oxytocin [known as the love hormone, oxytocin is released when people make deep social connections], the higher the empathy. The higher the empathy, the deeper the connection."[51]

Levin continues, describing eight simple ways you can create a culture of trust, according to Zak:

1. Recognize excellence
2. Induce "challenge" stress
3. Empower employees to choose their work patterns and habits
4. Give employees a voice in their own job design
5. Communicate often
6. Intentionally build relationships
7. Facilitate whole person growth
8. Show vulnerability[52]

These are all core values of extraordinary entrepreneurship and are all things you can do without a lot of time, a big budget, or a fancy degree. All it takes is intentional awareness on the part of leaders. In the next chapter, we'll take this a step forward when I share several strategies to help you invest in and empower your people. Team member empowerment built on top of a culture of trust can be virtually unstoppable in business. It can catch loops before they barely slow you down and keep your company moving toward a vision of success that makes you proud.

Failing Forward With Fried Chicken

One of the most famous "suck to success" stories is that of Harland Sanders, better known to fried chicken fans as Colonel Sanders of Kentucky Fried Chicken. Sanders was 65 years old when he started what would become one of the most iconic brands in the restaurant industry. At the time, he had one restaurant in North Corbin, Kentucky, which was located on a major road, bringing him plenty of traffic from hungry travelers. But nearby interstate highway construction rerouted his customers around his business, so they no longer drove past his location. Revenue dropped so much that he was eventually forced to sell his business.

After locking the doors for the last time, Sanders took the one asset he had left—his mother's chicken recipe—and went on a mission to sell the recipe. He took his meager savings and $105 per month Social Security check and hit the road, traversing the country from one diner to the next, cooking the recipe for restaurant owners.

The Colonel was so determined that he slept in the back of his car. He found great pleasure in teaching potential customers how to make his recipe using his unique techniques. But he was struggling to make his first sale. He was failing. Harland Sanders needed to reframe failure. So, what did he do? Like many of the greatest success stories in history, he naturally followed what I've turned into the simple E-4 Process I shared with you in Chapter 4:

- He **identified what wasn't working.** Originally, Sanders turned his mother's recipe into fried chicken. Over time, he realized that frying the chicken didn't differentiate him enough in the eyes of restaurant owners, so he began pressure-cooking the chicken. That allowed the food to be processed quicker and gave it a unique flavor. Quicker food preparation and unique flavor are two high-value qualities in the restaurant world.
- He **set an intention (not an expectation)** about how he would profit from his recipe. He had learned his lesson from having all of his business income tied to one location, so he focused on making money from multiple locations. His pitch was simple. Restaurant owners would pay him four cents from every order of chicken sold, creating recurring revenue for himself without the risk of one construction project taking his income to zero.
- He **planned and took action** by hitting the road, demonstrating the process, and cooking the chicken himself for restaurant owners.
- He **got help, iterated, pivoted, and repeated** by getting feedback from restaurant owners and adjusting the process from frying the chicken to pressure cooking it, a

big breakthrough. The Colonel and his now famous recipe were rejected 1,009 times. But he didn't give up. He got feedback, tweaked, and moved forward, getting feedback from restaurant owner after restaurant owner. Talk about a lot of feedback!

In 1952, the "Kentucky Fried Chicken" recipe was franchised for the first time in Salt Lake City, Utah. Ten years later, the Colonel experienced significant success and the company soon grew to more than 600 franchised outlets. At 73, he sold what would eventually be called just KFC to investors for $2 million (more than $15 million in today's dollars). He became a salaried brand spokesman. Today, KFC is the world's fourth-largest restaurant chain with more than 20,000 locations across the globe. And Colonel Sanders' image still appears on its logo.

Sanders failed, and failed, and failed, and failed. Or did he? In just eight years, beginning with his 65th year on Earth, Sanders got rejected more than 1,000 times, but he ended up earning the equivalent of a $15 million payday, plus the revenue from franchises along the way and spokesperson income after the sale. He might be one of the best examples of the "win or learn" and "fail-forward" mentality in history.

Creating Margin By Focusing On Margins

The last piece of the puzzle for navigating the looping line of success is to give yourself and your team some margin—and I mean that in both senses of the word. In life, having "margin" means we have some flexibility; we are not living right up on the edge so our business collapses when one thing goes wrong.

That margin will help us in many ways, even beyond disaster prevention. Having margin allows us to say no to problem clients. It gives us flexibility to pivot away from parts of our businesses that are not fulfilling to something more fulfilling and profitable. And, importantly, it gives us the flexibility to make time for personal and family priorities.

I learned from Greg early on that getting the margin we need as entrepreneurs comes from improving "margins" in our business. This might be the most valuable lesson I learned from working with my brother. Of course, I knew it was important to be profitable. But profitable is really not the same as improving margins, although improving margins does generally increase profits.

I still remember how hopeful I felt—for the first time in a long time—when Greg first helped me start focusing on margins. That was a special moment I'll carry with me for the rest of my life. So, although I have helped a lot of entrepreneurs get margin by improving margins, I thought there would be no better person to join me in sharing about this important subject than Greg, himself.

Greg is an expert in turning around companies and has become known as a magician when it comes to improving gross margins. In fact, his most impactful presentation he conducts for struggling companies is one he calls "Margin Magic." I asked him to share a little bit of his magic show with us to help you create margin through improving margins at your company. (I guess that makes me his magician's assistant, and I'm fine with that.)

Margin Magic By Greg Palmer

If there were one metric we can focus on that would ensure all of the most important performance metrics are improved, it would be gross margins. Even better, it's both simple yet powerful. You don't need to be a CPA to understand your gross margins. Yet, when you improve gross margins, it automatically improves all the more sophisticated metrics.

Here's how it works.

Simply put, gross margins are the percentage of revenue above the Cost of Goods Sold (COGS), which represents the business expenses required to produce goods. This generally includes raw materials and wages for labor required to produce or assemble products or to deliver services. It does not include business expenses that are not related to the production and delivery of the goods, such as rent, utilities, and marketing expenses.

The formula to calculate your gross margins percentage is as follows: [revenue minus COGS] divided by revenue. So, if your revenue is $5 million and your COGS is $4 million, your gross margin percentage would be calculated as follows: $5 million - $4 millions = $1 million, divided by $5 million. Thus, your gross margin percentage would be 20 percent.

A 20 percent gross margin is fairly healthy for most businesses, but it really depends on the type of business it is. Todd's business was operating at less than that, at around 15 percent, when I first got involved in his business. That meant he had very little wiggle room to make a mistake before his profit would get squeezed. It took him $85 in COGS to generate $100 in revenue. He was focused on high-volume, low-margin accounts, placing a lot of unskilled labor, and competing against larger companies. He wasn't able to add that much of a markup on top of the people he was placing. He was, as they say in the South, between a rock and a hard place.

Todd's other operating expenses were also significant when compared to his gross margin. We realized that his EBITDA (earnings before interest, taxes, depreciation, and amortization) were running only 5 percent as a percent of revenue, which is relatively low. In Todd's case, we realized that if he could increase his gross margin percentage by 1 percent—or $0.20 per hour—to just a 16 percent gross profit (GP), we could increase his profits by 20 percent. That's all it would take—20 cents per hour. Done!

When we looked at the numbers that way, Todd felt a great sense of relief. So many different variables impact gross margins. Surely, we could find 1 percent somewhere. And we did, pretty easily. In Todd's case, we found it by committing to finding a more profitable niche in the staffing world that allowed him to charge a premium placement fee, immediately boosting gross margins. In less than nine months, he went from 16 percent GP to 26 percent GP. Abracadabra, Margin Magic, his EBITDA doubled!

Almost immediately, Todd's cash flow improved by leaps and bounds. Even better, he knew exactly what variables to work on improving to increase margins and cash flow even more. Over time, even micro-changes to each variable add up:

- You can increase your pricing by a small percentage.
- You can change your focus from large accounts to small, high-margin accounts.
- You can change suppliers to save money on raw materials.
- You can substitute raw materials, often finding a better solution at a lower cost.
- You can adjust staffing to reduce labor costs.
- You can automate parts of the process to reduce the need for human intervention.

The opportunities are virtually limitless, and the impact is extraordinary when you focus your attention on improving gross margins.

If Greg's Margin Magic seems almost too simple, that's why it's so good. It can literally make profits appear—seemingly out of nowhere—with no sleight of hand, just a few adjustments to pricing and COGS. That's why "margins" have become one of the lowest-hanging fruits I've found to help create "EBITDA Margin" in the businesses and lives of the people I coach. It's one of the first things I help them with from a business strategy perspective.

Here are some of the steps I work through with entrepreneurs to help them get started. First, I work with them to understand their current situation. This includes:

- segmenting the business into logical groupings (e.g., different products or services or different account sizes),
- understanding the costs for each grouping, and whether they are improving or getting worse,
- analyzing pricing for each grouping based on relevant data (e.g., competitor research or unique selling proposition), and
- analyzing compensation rates for the entrepreneur and the staff.

Then we follow five steps to improving margins, which I got directly from Greg. Having these steps in place helps us move forward methodically and consistently:

- Conduct a SWOT analysis for your business. What are your Strengths, Weaknesses, Opportunities, and Threats?
- Create a plan. What variables will we look to impact and how?
- Set up key performance indicators, or KPIs. How will we measure progress along the way?
- Schedule regular communications with your team. Remember, consistent and clear communication builds trust and accountability. Be the ATV leader.
- Track, adjust, and tackle the problem areas. Just like the fourth step in the E-4 Process, we need to get help, iterate, and adjust as we go. If you get stuck, you can go straight to the E-4 Process itself to identify what's not working, set a new intention, get help, plan, and pivot, and then iterate and adjust.

If you brand yourself, get comfortable with failure, create a culture of trust, and then regularly practice Margin Magic, you will be well on your way to creating a rock-solid foundation for your business. With that in place, you'll be ready to empower your team to lift your business to heights you may never have thought possible. That's what we'll talk about in the next chapter.

Insights

- Success is a looping, nonlinear path.
- Without adversity, growth is impossible.
- As a professional or entrepreneur, you are a brand. Know thyself.
- Giving your customer "free things" builds trust. Trust builds followers, and followers convert into loyal customers.
- Margins create financial flexibility for you and your business. Practice Margin Magic and you'll build a strong financial foundation to lift your business to new heights.

Questions For Reflection

- How can you move your margins?
- What is so important to you that you would be willing to fail 1,009 times to make it happen?
- Do you have a culture of trust within your organization?
- What is your plan to give away things for free?
- Who is your ideal client avatar? Does your brand attract this client?

Action Steps

- See stress, adversity, and failures as gifts and growth opportunities.
- Invest in creating a culture of trust within your teams and organization.
- Be a servant-leader to your ideal customer, giving them several things away for free and earn their loyalty.

Additional Resources

Adams, Scott. *How to Fail at Almost Everything and Still Win Big: Kind of the Story of My Life.* New York: Portfolio/Penguin, 2013.

Gabor, Deb. *Branding Is Sex: Get Your Customers Laid and Sell the Hell Out of Anything.* Austin: Lioncrest Publishing, 2016.

Gabor, Deb. *Irrational Loyalty: Building a Brand That Thrives in Turbulent Times.* Austin: Lioncrest Publishing, 2019.

Krimitsos, Chris. *Start Ugly: A Timeless Tale about Innovation & Change*. Tampa: Shake Creative, 2019.

Pulizzi, Joe. *Content Inc.: How Entrepreneurs Use Content to Build Massive Audiences and Create Radically Successful Businesses*. New York: McGraw-Hill Education, 2016.

Zak, Paul J. *The Trust Factor: The Science of Creating High-Performance Companies*. New York: AMACOM, 2017.

Also visit ExtraordinaryAdvisors.com for more exclusive coaching tips.

Chapter 6

Empowering Yourself With People

"What makes us weird also makes us wonderful. What makes us weak also makes us strong."
— David Rendall, Speaker & Author, The Freak Factor: Discovering Uniqueness by
Flaunting Weakness

From the outside, Tom Schwab might look like one of the "lucky ones" in business. In 2015, he founded a company called Interview Valet, the first high-end service of its kind that helped business owners find lucrative marketing opportunities through strategic podcast guest appearances.

Tom also wrote *Podcast Guest Profits: Grow Your Business with a Targeted Interview Strategy*, which he calls "the bible of podcast guesting." When I first met Tom, he had already built an impressive business. He was making good money and helping a lot of people. But he was doing way too much in his business and that slowed him down. As I mentioned in Chapter 1, Tom was manually entering payroll for his company every Sunday night, for example.

When Tom hired me to coach him, he immediately struck me as someone who was sitting on a pile of silver a few steps away from a goldmine. We needed to free up his time to do what he did best—building relationships with clients and empowering his people. I challenged Tom to look at his current leadership team. Were they aligned with his vision? Were they doing what it took to drive the business forward? Relatively soon after that conversation, Tom leaned into the uncomfortable decision of letting go of some senior leaders, replacing them with a new crop of aligned employees who embodied the core values of the organization. We needed him to get out of his own way and empower his new people to perform. After doing so, his revenue grew 70 percent in the first year. Thanks to some Margin

Magic, his net profits jumped 500 percent during that time. Yes, in the first year.

When people see Tom today, he looks like a "lucky one" who was first to arrive in a growing industry. In fact, the real reason for Tom's success is his extraordinary ability to work with people. If you spend five minutes on the phone with him, I know you'll immediately agree.

"The richness of your life is the riches of your relationships," he says. "One of the worst things you could do to anybody is put them in solitary confinement. It's considered cruel and unusual punishment in many countries, but yet we do it to ourselves and especially as business owners. We put our heads down and just work. But what if we were to just pick up our heads and realize that those relationships we have and those people around us want to help?"

Tom has also grown to accept conflict in relationships. "It's OK to challenge and push each other to be better," he says. "It doesn't have to be artificial harmony. Once you go through a struggle with somebody, you typically come out on the other side stronger." This was a huge breakthrough for him.

While the Margin Magic we worked on together created the opportunities for Tom's 70 percent revenue growth and 500 percent profit growth in one year, the truth is, he would never have been able to generate the revenue and profit growth without replacing underperforming staff and empowering his new leadership team to execute and perform.

How do Tom and other entrepreneurs do it? We'll explore that in this chapter, because the truth is that your systems will only be as effective as the people implementing them. If you're the bottleneck, your business will be limited by how much can get through you. If you don't empower your team to perform, your business will be limited by how restrictive you are on your team. But if you start with a solid foundation, like the one we built in Chapter 5, and then break the bottleneck and empower your team to execute, the sky's the limit.

Staff Underperformance Is A Symptom, Not The Problem

Having the right people in the right positions with the right tools to perform can be an absolute game-changer for any company. Yet almost every entrepreneur I work with comes to me listing staff challenges as one of their major complaints. Their staff won't work hard enough. Their performance is inconsistent. The list goes on. Over the years, I've heard every variation of "My staff is my problem" you can imagine.

While I certainly empathize with that feeling, it's wrong. Staff underperformance might be *a* problem but it's never *the* problem in a business. It's just the symptom of the real problem, which is often a combination of the lack of ATV leadership, having the wrong people on your staff or in the wrong position, and not empowering your team members to perform.

In other words, almost without exception, staff problems are really leadership problems. You might not be practicing ATV leadership. You might not have built a solid foundation that gives you margin and builds deep relationships and a culture of trust. You might have hired the wrong people. You might have hired the right people but put them in the wrong position. Or, you might have hired the right people, put them in the right position, but failed to empower them to perform. When staff is the perceived problem, it's almost always the person who chooses and leads them who is the real problem.

So how do you fix it? First, you need to understand yourself as a leader better. If you've been working on your ATV leadership and executing the other strategies so far, that's a start. Let's go a little deeper, though. Ask yourself some tough questions:
- How do you see yourself? Are you an effective leader? How do you think your team members see you?
- Do you struggle to make tough choices? Do you keep people around longer than you should?
- Do you avoid uncomfortable conversations?
- Do you feel like you are trying to be all things to all people?

Keep digging:

- How are you handling the blocking and tackling of running a business?
- What are the key performance indicators that matter to you? Do your team members know about them? Do they know how to impact them? Do they have the tools they need to succeed?
- Are people held accountable? How?
- Are you running weekly meetings and daily huddles?

If you feel slightly uncomfortable with any of these questions, your team is likely not reaching their full potential. That's the bad news. The good news is you can help your team reach their full potential by empowering yourself to lead them well and giving them the tools, training, and resources to perform. And if you've done the work from the first five chapters, you've built the leadership and business foundation upon which to build something extraordinary.

For the rest of this chapter, I'll share strategies for you to cultivate psychologically safe workplaces, implement a good jobs strategy, and build deeper relationships with your team members to achieve long-lasting growth.

Tom Schwab on Building Relationships In Business

When reaching out to someone, internally or externally, remember that each conversation moves a relationship in one direction or another. No conversation is simply a transaction. It leaves an impression and either strengthens or weakens trust.

Whatever we do in our business must be a win-win for the people involved. Look how you can add value to people. Invest in helping them succeed. And be open to different perspectives from people who want to help you.

Being one step removed from the interactions between customers and your business gives leaders an important perspective. But that perspective comes with the significant challenge of being one step removed from what your employees and customers experience on a day-to-day basis. Thus, treat every customer and team member as people with an important perspective that you don't have, even if you spent years working in your business.

Your best ideas for the future often come from employees and customers who remain involved in the day-to-day operations of your business. They are the ones experiencing what it's like to do business with you in the present and the future, even if you have years of experience working on the front lines in the past.

Investing In Your Employees For Greater Profits

There's an old saying in real estate investing that "the money is made on the purchase and not on the sale." In other words, if you choose the right property and pay the right price, you will be set up for success. But if you choose the wrong property or overpay, it will take a lot of time, money, or effort to eke out a profit.

A similar principle applies when building a team. Specifically, how you find and onboard them will make a big difference in how they perform. If you find the right people, structure their pay well, and give them the tools, training, and support they need, they can be off to the races. If not, you'll make your life a lot harder than it needs to be. Avoid hiring just for skill sets. You're not hiring a robot; you're hiring a person. Look for someone who fits in with your company's core values and has the capabilities to perform and the work ethic to grow. You can't change someone's DNA. You can't change their attitude. But you can invest in training and support to adjust their skills. That's why it's so important to hire the right candidates for your culture and not just the candidate with the most relevant experience.

If you find yourself surrounded by underperforming employees, there's hope. Leaning into, not away from, a few tough decisions can make a world of difference. Just shift the way you screen, select, and onboard team members in the future so you stop the bleeding while you work on setting up your current employees for success.

If you find yourself with staff issues, you're not alone. Many seasoned business professionals struggle in the area of human capital. For example, a lot of companies habitually start new employees at or near minimum wage, provide poorly designed on-the-job training, put new employees on second or third shifts, or give new employees a mixed-hours schedule. Or they quickly get new employees working and treat them like robots without giving them any context to their tasks or sharing how their participation contributes to the company's vision and purpose.

Contrast that with a company that is willing to offer slightly more than market pay for people with proven track records and the right attitude and then invests a little bit of time and money into their first week on the job. During that week, the leaders and coworkers all talk with the new team member about the company vision and their favorite feel-good story about the impact of their work. They give the new team member high-quality tools, hands-on training, and access to a knowledge base with videos and other guides about the company, its culture, and the tasks assigned to them.

Which company do you think would be more confident in their team? It's a no-brainer. The second company would outperform the first every time— and they could do it with fewer people and lower overall labor costs when you factor in turnover and the number of low performers you'd have to hire to replicate the production of the high performers. When comparing successful companies, culture and continuous training eat strategy for breakfast! Poor treatment, poverty-level wages, poorly designed training, chaotic scheduling, and a lack of culture and purpose is a surefire way to drive away your top performers and get the poor performers to do just enough to not get fired while they keep their eyes open for a better job opportunity.

Over the short-term, cutting labor costs is sometimes necessary and stomached by team members. During the Great Recession of the late 2000s, or in the midst of the coronavirus pandemic, many companies temporarily cut wages across the board to save long-term jobs. But making it a way of life to drive down wages and reduce costs by providing subpar equipment and training is a poor long-term plan.

This "doing more with less" had its day during the mid-20th century, perhaps, but it has clearly run its course. And even in recessionary markets, companies are willing to pay for top talent these days because they know they're worth it. In fact, many companies take advantage of recessionary markets to lure top performers from struggling companies with increasingly creative offers and using its culture, purpose, and team member support as additional value to entice top performers.

This doesn't mean you need to just throw all your money at staff, either. Attracting and supporting top performers doesn't just save you money by helping you do more with fewer people. It saves you money in many other ways, too. In fact, attracting top performers through culture, purpose, pay, and support can help you reduce costs in several ways. For example, consider the findings published by MIT professor Zeynep Ton. In *The Good Jobs Strategy: How the Smartest Companies Invest in Employees to Lower Costs and Boost Profits,* Ton argues that a company can adopt a low-cost strategy that promotes investment in employees.[53] She says treating employees as real high-value assets in which companies invest resources can foster an environment that leads to higher profit, improved efficiencies, and better customer service. This happens because everyone on the team understands the context of the work and buys into the purpose behind it. They know what to do, why they're doing it, and how to get the job done. And they're working for a company that sees them as valuable contributors and gives them the tools and training they need to perform.[54]

To support her research, Ton examines the example of Home Depot in the early 2000s. At the end of 2000, Home Depot cut staffing levels and increased the percentage of part-time workers to reduce labor costs (and boost profits). While those moves worked in the short term, in the long term, they caused Home Depot's customer service to deteriorate. That led to a significant drop in sales for the home improvement retailer. "Making a retail store, or any service environment, hum," writes Ton, "requires not only employees who are capable, knowledgeable, motivated, and sufficient in number but also close attention to the design of operations—what these employees do all day, and how they do it."[55]

Contrast Home Depot's experiment with Zappos, long famous for its continued commitment to employees. In fact, the company is open about its commitment, even posting seven Zappos amenities on its blog[56] that boost employee happiness for everyone to see. I've outlined them for you below, along with a short explanation from the article:

1. A Relaxed Dress Code
"With the booming success of trendsetters like Apple, Facebook, and yes, even Zappos, it's clear that 'casual corporate' won't hold your company back but will help your employees feel empowered to move it forward."

2. Team Buildings
"Giving teams time to relax and get to know each other is crucial to productivity."

3. Office Library
"If you want employees who are truly all on the same page, try giving them the pages! An office library isn't necessarily a quiet room where people go to read (though, that's not a bad idea) but a collection of books your employees can borrow from the company. Business books, reference books, books on improving writing or coding skills; these resources can only benefit your employees."

4. Internal Currency
"Zappos.com employees give each other 'Zollars' to reward everything from performance to holding a door open for someone. This Monopoly-esque money can be redeemed in its Zollar Store, a place filled with swag, raffles, and the newest tech toys. Not only does this allow employees to reward one another, but it provides one more incentive for your coworkers to be their best."

5. Discounted Food and Drink
Zappos provides "a chef and talented kitchen staff who makes gourmet meals for employees at a low cost. We all need to eat, and giving discounts on necessities can undoubtedly boost morale and trust within a company."

6. Relaxation Areas
"Designated places for employees to nap during breaks and lunches may seem like a luxury, but longer workdays are making it a necessity. Fact: this is a simple and effective way to improve the health, happiness, and performance of your employees."

7. A Place to Be Themselves
"No matter where people work or what they do there, the best way for them

to find happiness in it is to feel as though they can be themselves. This goes beyond casual dress. It means allowing them to put a creative spin on their work, giving time and attention to their opinion, and helping the office feel like a place they belong."

You might not be running Zappos, but you can implement simple, low-cost policies that promote these seven principles in your organization. I have yet to meet a single entrepreneur who was leading a team and couldn't. Often, all it takes is a little creativity and a commitment to a more fulfilled, productive workplace for both employees and leaders.

How else can you set up your team members for success? Here are some more suggestions from Professor Ton.

Your Good Jobs Strategy

You've invested in improving your mind-set, leadership, and intention setting. You've committed to identifying top staff candidates and paying them appropriately. And you have started putting team-building policies in place like Zappos. Now it's time to structure your business to set up your team members for success. In her book, *The Good Jobs Strategy*, Professor Ton shares several strategies for lowering costs and boosting profits by investing in employees.

Here, I want to share four strategies I've used with many of my clients to help them structure their business and operations to set their team members up for success. Anyone can make these business structure and operations adjustments to empower their team to perform.

1. Limit Offerings and Products/Services

Sometimes the problem with performance is you are asking your team members to become experts in way too many offerings. More products that require customer service. More things to go wrong. More details to manage.

Professor Ton uses the warehouse store Costco as an example of a company that offers many products but only a few brands from each category. It also offers limited promotions and shorter hours.

If you're trying to be everything to everyone, your employees are likely bearing the burden and underperforming as a result. Look for ways to limit offerings and reduce complex promotion strategies. Consider reducing your niche even further (see Chapter 5 for help doing so). Your team will thank you and your brand will become clearer and more specific to the outside world.

2. Standardize and Empower
After assessing offers and promotions, look for ways to systematize operations. Be sure to involve your team members in the process of doing so, too. Ask the frontline staff what bottlenecks they are facing in their jobs. What is impacting their ability to provide a great customer experience? In the end, the goal is to create systems and processes for employees to make better, more consistent decisions and achieve better, more consistent performance. Finally, encourage your team members to suggest improvements to existing systems and new systems you can put in place to further help them perform.

3. Cross Train
Years ago, specialists were the most coveted team members. Today, while specialty is still appreciated, versatile team members are coveted. Training your team across multiple functions will help your organization in many ways. It allows you to shift staffing based on needs and workflow. You create team members who no longer carry the mind-set of "That's not in my job description." And it helps your team members understand the full context and impact of their tasks, which helps everyone perform at their best.

4. Operate with "Slack"
It's counterintuitive, but Professor Ton suggests scheduling more team members than you need to meet the demands of the day. Doing so immediately benefits your leaders. They can focus on leading and training team members instead of putting out fires all day caused by understaffing. This *margin* (there's that word again) will also allow you and other leaders to focus on improving systems and processes and make other higher-level decisions.

Additionally, overstaffing reduces the need for overtime, saving costs and avoiding employee burnout. It also improves customer service because your team members won't be rushing from task to task, and the additional staff will give you flexibility to move your cross-trained team members around to where attention is needed most on a day-to-day basis.

In the end, these four "Good Jobs Strategy" operational practices help companies better control costs; utilize employees as assets, not expenses; and boost satisfaction and loyalty among staff and customers. That's a recipe for higher profits and leaders who become more and more free to focus on higher-level initiatives.

Cultivating Healthy Organizations

As you and your team free up for higher-level initiatives, the first one I encourage you to work on is improving organizational health and culture. That will not only help you grow your bottom line but it will also help your organization start to police itself so you no longer have to get involved in day-to-day operations as often. Your organization will be strong, and your team members will know exactly what behavior is acceptable and unacceptable. And if someone continually acts out of line, they will quickly find themselves looking for other opportunities because that behavior will not be tolerated. The stronger your core values become, the more likely it is for your team members—in addition to the leaders—to police them. No matter how it comes to your attention, when someone continually acts in violation of your core values, you need to let them go—as soon as you see that it's a pattern and not a one-time error. If you don't, your company's core values will weaken, and you risk your best team members looking for greener pastures.

> Your core values cannot only be visible on your website and office walls. They must be visible in how you hire and fire. If someone continually acts out of line with your core values, you must let them go for the good of the organization.

Author Patrick Lencioni is one of my favorite business and team management writers around. Pick up any of his books and you'll find it to be an interesting and helpful read. When it comes to organizational health, I'd highly recommend *The Four Obsessions of an Extraordinary Executive,*

in which he shares the following four disciplines of a healthy organization:
- Building and maintaining a cohesive leadership team
- Creating organizational clarity
- Over-communicating organizational clarity
- Reinforcing organizational clarity through human systems[57]

These four disciplines incorporate some of what we already talked about when it comes to branding, limiting consumer offerings, and communicating with team members. But, as Lencioni explains, executives are often blind to the most corrosive aspect of leadership teams: politics and a lack of trust. "This blindness occurs because what executives believe are small disconnects between themselves and their peers actually look like major rifts to people deeper in the organization," he writes. "And when those people deeper in the organization try to resolve the differences among themselves, they often become engaged in bloody and time-consuming battles, with no possibility for resolution. And all of these occur because leaders higher in the organization failed to work out minor issues, usually out of fear of conflict."[58] Thus, we don't just work on these disciplines to put our team members in a position to perform. We also do so with the intention of building trust and improving culture within the four walls of our organization.

So what does it look like to create organizational clarity? As Lencioni explains, having organizational strategy means a company has aligned all of its resources, especially human ones. "When employees at all levels share a common understanding of where the company is headed," he writes, "what success looks like, whom their competitors are, and what needs to be achieved to claim victory, there is a remarkably low level of wasted time and energy and a powerful sense of traction."[59] Furthermore, artificial harmony among leadership and team members is forbidden. Leadership forces difficult and necessary conversations among staff to foster a healthy workplace.

It also changes how we hire and evaluate team members. Specifically, it allows companies to skip the generic hiring practices and performance reviews. Instead, it lets leaders focus on having "ongoing dialogue around how employees can align their behaviors around the organization's clarity."[60] In other words, you have less of a need for formal performance reviews because you address any issues and pivot whenever needed, even on a daily basis. And as your organization begins to police itself, issues are often addressed at the staff level in a healthy way.

Creating Extraordinary Cultures

When you're ready to focus on creating extraordinary cultures, it's typically a time to celebrate. It means you've started the hard work of improving yourself and investing in your team, and now you're ready to invest in creating a workplace that builds its own identity. You will no longer only be building a collection of systems, people, and a brand that connects those people with the outside world. You will be building an entity independent of the people, processes, and brand that helps everyone involved in your company thrive.

When I first started digging my way out of debt, "culture" wasn't even a thing in the business world. That said, there was no denying that my company would be described as having a toxic culture by today's standards. And I now know all the ill effects that having a toxic culture has on a company. I also know how important it is to not stop after we improve ourselves as leaders, build a team of high performers, and create systems and a supportive environment to help everyone succeed. We must also intentionally build a culture that continues to support what we have built moving forward. When we do, our culture will help drive us forward, like we're sailing with the wind at our backs every time we walk through the door.

"Group culture is one of the most powerful forces on the planet," explains Dan Coyle, author of *The Culture Code: The Secrets of Highly Successful Groups*. "We sense its presence inside successful businesses, championship teams, and thriving families, and we sense when it's absent or toxic. We can measure its impact on the bottom line. (A strong culture increases net income 756 percent over 11 years, according to a Harvard study of more than 200 companies.) Yet the inner workings of culture remain mysterious. We all want strong culture in our organizations, communities, and families. We all know that it works. We just don't know quite how it works."[61]

Coyle spent four years examining eight of the world's most successful groups, from a professional basketball team to a comedy troupe. From his research, he observed that it only takes three skills to build cultures that thrive:

- Building psychological safety
- Sharing vulnerability
- Establishing purpose[62]

As with cultivating healthy organizations, these three skills might sound familiar. That's good news for entrepreneurs. You don't need to do anything complicated or new to create an extraordinary culture. You just need to focus your work on building safety, sharing vulnerability, and establishing purpose at a macro-organizational level—and not just with direct reports, with team building, or with branding. Coyle's work can help you do that.

Building psychological safety in this context involves creating a culture that encourages connection and generates bonds of belonging within the greater organization. In other words, a new team member won't just be a member of the small clique of people with whom they interact on a daily basis. They become proud members of your organization, wearing their association with you as a badge of honor.

Sharing vulnerability in this context involves getting into habits of taking mutual risk to drive trusting cooperation in your organization. For example, consider how discussions around the conference room or team Zoom meetings are intended to play out versus how they actually play out. When someone suggests a "bad" idea, do you or others reply with a roll of the eyes or simply shut it down as a bad idea? Or do you dig deeper to discover their reasoning, which could spur an idea that might actually work?

If you do the former, it's only a matter of time before people stop offering suggestions, and your best innovations might never come to light. If you do the latter, you will encourage people to bring forth their greatest ideas. Because the best ideas are never the first iteration, consider even making a formal "There are no bad ideas" policy to foster free-flow sharing of ideas in your company.

Establishing purpose in this context helps create an organization-wide narrative of shared goals and values. It gives team members a North Star, a guiding principle, and an understanding of why their work matters to the outside world. Having a greater purpose can motivate people in even the most seemingly menial tasks to work harder and enjoy their work.

"The three skills work together from the bottom up," writes Coyle, "first building group connection and then channeling it into action."

The results you will achieve from investing in culture will strengthen over time in measurable ways, including higher morale, lower turnover, and even increased production and profits.

The Power Of Cross-Pollination

"My dad grew up in inner-city Chicago. When he moved his family out to the suburbs, he planted every fruit tree he could on his small lot. He took care of the pear tree, the apple tree, and the cherry tree. But they never produced fruit. After a couple of years, our next-door neighbor, a farmer who had moved into the suburbs laughed at my father's struggle.

"The farmer explained to my father that it didn't matter how much light and water his plants got. His trees would never produce fruit because there was no cross-pollination. For fruit to grow, pollen from the male part of the plant has to be transferred to the female part of the plant, often by birds or insects. Most fruit trees, including the ones my father planted, require cross-pollination from multiple trees to start producing fruit.

"It didn't matter what my father did; his land wasn't big enough to plant multiple trees of each kind, so he would never produce fruit. Fortunately, the neighbor was nice enough to plant similar trees on his land and, the next year, all the trees produced fruit.

"I think it's the same way within our businesses and our lives. We're never going to bear fruit in our lives if we just stay in our cubicles. We need to intentionally cross-pollinate, bring people around us, and empower them to do their best work and share their ideas with us. If we do, we will expose ourselves to new ideas and ways of doing things and everyone will bear more fruit."
— Tom Schwab[63]

Foster Teams That Support Psychological Safety

When I help leaders work on creating healthy cultures, one of the biggest challenges they encounter is the concept of building teams that support psychological safety within the organization.

We are living in a business world that is going through mass transformation regarding human capital. Manufacturers, for example, do not have enough of the "right employees" and, with seven million job openings in the United States (as of December 2019), employees have more job options than ever before.

Typically, the "right employees" are defined as the highest performers within an organization. How can manufacturers create an environment for the "right employees" to thrive? The need for high-performing employees cuts across all sectors of employment. In a two-year study of its internal workforce, Google asked, What makes a high performing team?[64] Largely, the answer was psychological safety, the belief that you won't be punished when you make a mistake.

Today, people work in teams more than ever before. One study, published in the *Harvard Business Review*, found that "the time spent by managers and employees in collaborative activities has ballooned by 50 percent or more" over the last two decades.[65]

To further understand psychological safety, let's look at the work of Harvard Business School Professor Amy Edmonson. She suggests that psychological safety has these components:
- First, it is a shared belief held by members of a team that the team is safe for interpersonal risk taking.
- Psychological safety is a sense of confidence that the team will not embarrass, reject, or punish someone for speaking up.
- It describes a team climate characterized by interpersonal trust and mutual respect in which people are comfortable being themselves.

How can your organization create psychological safety? Consider changing the behaviors and norms within your corporate culture. Here are four things psychologically safe organizations practice:
- Approach conflict as a collaborator, not an adversary. True success

at work comes from a win-win result. When we experience a perceived loss, this loss triggers attempts to reestablish fairness through competition, criticism, or disengagement. Start with the mind-set of achieving a mutually desired outcome, which will quell our instinctual fight-or-flight reaction.

- Speak human to human—a "just like me" mind-set. We all have universal needs such as respect, competence, social status, and autonomy. When you are having an intense negotiation, for example, the other party is just like you and aims to walk away happy. This person has beliefs, perspectives, and opinions, just like you. This person has hopes, anxieties, and vulnerabilities, just like you, and this person wants to feel respected, appreciated, and competent, just like you.

- Anticipate reactions and plan countermoves. Before you engage with a coworker, proactively think of how the other person will react to you. Lean into uncomfortable conversations head-on by preparing for likely reactions. Think about your main points. What are three ways the recipient of your message is possibly going to react? How will you handle each of those scenarios?

- Replace blame with curiosity. Borrow a technique from renowned marriage counselor John Gottman. His work shows that blame and criticism reliably escalate conflict, leading to defensiveness and eventually to disengagement.[66] Adopt a learning mind-set, with an awareness that you don't have all the facts. He suggests you state the problematic behavior or outcome as an observation, and use factual, neutral language. If you have an employee who is underperforming, you may say, "In the past two months, there's been a noticeable drop in your participation during meetings and progress appears to be slowing on your project."

Engage employees in an exploration. For example, "I imagine there are multiple factors at play. Perhaps we could uncover what they are together?" Ask for solutions. The people who are responsible for creating a problem often hold the keys to solving it. Ask directly, "What do you think needs to happen here?" or "What would be your ideal scenario?" Another question leading to solutions is "How could I support you?"

If you create this sense of psychological safety within your organization, you can expect to see higher levels of engagement, increased motivation to tackle difficult problems, more learning and development opportunities, and better performance.

Together with building a healthy organization and investing in your team members like the assets they are, you will build a well-oiled machine full of high-caliber team members who are positioned to perform. In the next chapter, we will turn to higher-level strategies for taking action and improving from feedback. These higher-level strategies will help us continue to grow while addressing challenges that arise as our companies start to scale. And they are even more important during the inevitable bad times we face as economies cycle between growth and contraction.

Insights
- Don't accept artificial harmony in the workplace. Lean into, not away from, tough conversations.
- People are key to any business.
- Psychologically safe work environments perform better.

Questions For Reflection
- What is your Good Jobs Strategy?
- Are you investing in key relationships (clients, employees, loved ones)? If you aren't, who should be on your list?
- Are you willing to invest in yourself and hire a coach?
- What is your leadership style? Is it delivering the results you seek?

Action Steps
- Employees are profit centers to an organization, not cost centers.
- Since culture is the key to recruiting and retaining employees, put culture as the main focus of the leadership team.
- Take the steps needed to continuously train and upskill your workforce.
- When dealing with people, leaders can create more trust and connectivity by approaching issues or problems with massive curiosity, not blame. "Tell me more" is a great way to get others to share what happened.
- Own your core values. Share your core values on your website and in your office. Hire and fire by them.
- Practice active listening. Listen to absorb first, respond second.

Additional Resources
Schwab, Thomas M. *Podcast Guest Profits: Grow Your Business with a Targeted Interview Strategy.* Interview Valet, 2016.

Ton, Zeynep. T*he Good Jobs Strategy: How the Smartest Companies Invest in Employees to Lower Costs and Boost Profits.* Boston: New Harvest, 2014.

Also visit ExtraordinaryAdvisors.com for more exclusive coaching tips.

Chapter 7

Leadership Strategies For
The Worst Of Times

"Obstacles don't have to stop you. If you run into a wall, don't turn around and give up. Figure out how to climb it, go through it, or work around it."
—Michael Jordan

In the introduction, I briefly mentioned that the United States typically goes through a recession about every ten years, almost like clockwork. In 2020, the COVID-19 pandemic shut down the entire global economy. From December 2007 through June 2009, we experienced the "Great Recession."

In 2001, we experienced a recession following the bursting of the dot-com bubble. Before that, speculative tech stocks helped us avoid a recession for 20 years, which is the longest period of economic growth in US history.

Between 1970 and 1982, we experienced four recessions. In fact, we experienced fourteen recessions between 1937 and 2020. Why do I bring up that doom and gloom? Because we can't just plan our businesses to operate when times are good. We need to also be able to perform when economies shrink. The strategies and tactics we've talked about thus far will help, of course. They strengthen our companies to help smooth out our looping lines of success. And that helps us limit the downside we face in good times and in bad.

However, we must also have a strategy in place for when times get tough—because it's not a matter of if; it's a matter of when. We will face micro-challenges, such as industry challenges, failed mergers, acquisitions, or business initiatives. And we will face macro-challenges, such as the inevitable recessions and—as we learned the hard way in 2020—pandemics.

And what if I told you that my coaching business doubled from March 2020 through October 2020, the height of uncertainty and economic contraction associated with the COVID-19 pandemic? It's true. I don't say that to brag, either. It's not about me. It's about the plan I put in place to strategize and take action in my coaching business for good times and bad.

That planning and strategy started with me walking my talk for years. I work consistently on my mind-set, being an ATV leader, and setting intentions, not expectations. I visit—and revisit—the E-4 Process every day, likely multiple times a day. I work hard to operate with strong margins that help me prevent small mistakes from becoming big problems. I surround myself with top-quality people and invest in giving them everything they need to support my clients and me. I built that foundation over a number of years. So, when the COVID-19 pandemic hit and shut down or postponed every speaking engagement I had booked, I had margin.

But I also had a plan. And by "plan," I don't mean I had a 35-step pandemic response plan. I didn't. Yet after a few moments (OK, days) of beating myself up, I regrouped and knew exactly what to do next. I doubled down on my why to improve lives and focused on being of service to others. Not only did it work but it also ended up being the most prosperous period of time in the history of my coaching business. Of course, I wouldn't wish for it to happen again. We experienced way too much pain, sickness, and death in the world. But because I was able to strategize and shift to taking action, I was able to turn a world of suck into a tremendous success.

In this chapter, I'll help you get a head start on pivoting the next time the direction of the wind turns for your business, either on a micro- or macro-level.

When Times Get Tough, Ask More Questions

Let's return for a moment to my own story. When I was $600,000 in debt, we were about two years away from the biggest economic contraction since the Great Depression. Looking back, I'm now grateful that my business collapsed when it did. Had I been able to hold on for two more years, there would have been *no way* I would have been able to avoid filing for bankruptcy protection.

As you might remember, the strategy that Greg and I put together to get me out of debt involved several moving parts. After identifying what wasn't working, we set our intention for me to get out of debt, just like the E-4 Process I shared in Chapter 4 suggests. We didn't know how we'd do it, but we knew I needed to make more money and get paid faster.

That intention led us to reduce how long my clients had to pay me from at least 45 days to less than 14 days. That reduced defaults, got cash coming in faster, and limited my downside if a client went broke. We also changed my staff and switched from hiring experienced staffing people to hiring for culture and core values. DNA, not résumé. We did a lot of work on the foundation of my business, implementing the same strategies I shared in the first six chapters of this book. Over the longer term, we shifted Diversified Industrial Staffing's niche to start placing higher-skilled labor, which would generate higher margins.

Unfortunately, by the time I started building traction in my new niche, the world was in the midst of the Great Recession of 2008 and 2009. But that didn't mean I could give up. The work I had done with Greg to that point made my business stable enough to tread water, but treading water wasn't the intention. The intention was to pay down my debt. The intention was to grow.

So what could I do? I couldn't force companies to hire people, but I could reach out to people in my niche to gather information and build relationships with them to be able to serve them well when things turned back around. After all, while all recessions are different, one thing they all have in common is they all end. And when they end, they are followed by economic growth (by definition . . . otherwise the recession wouldn't have ended). So I knew it was only a matter of time when companies needed the type of staff I wanted to place.

I created a strategy around my intention of paying down that debt that involved reaching out to companies in the niche I was moving toward. I would try to either place people then, which was unlikely, or I would build relationships with the people so I could then place people when the economy turned back around. Part of the strategy involved finding companies that would still hire people during the recession. That was as hard to do as you might expect. I didn't know these companies. But my secondary purpose became to build relationships and strengthen my pitch for when things turned. A typical call would go something like this:

"I know we're in a recession," I'd say. "And I realize you're not hiring anybody right now."

"No, not talking about hiring anybody," she'd reply, "but thanks for calling."

"Well, before I let you go, let me ask you: If you could hire only one person when you come out of the recession, or only one skill set, what would that be?"

And she would pause and say, "You know, if I could just find a CNC machinist who could program in Mazak Mazatrol, I'd actually hire them immediately. In fact, if I could find them today, even though we're on a hiring freeze, I could convince the owners to hire that person right now."

I'd then thank her for her time and get off the phone.

Great! Now I had some feedback.

That became our script: "If you could hire only one person when you come out of the recession, or only one skill set, what would that be?" My team and I kept calling companies and asking that question over and over again. Every time, we'd make notes of the feedback and report back to each other. We were looking for patterns, looking to see where there was an increased demand for talent but a diminished supply of workers in that zone of demand.

We kept our eyes on the prize. I had to get out of debt somehow. I was buying time, but, as the leader, I also had developed a strategy. It might not bear fruit right away, but many businesses I called told me of at least one position they would hire immediately, so I had hope. If I could find people to fill those "right now" positions, I could get in with these companies and grow from there.

The strategy worked well. One of the reasons it did was because I was doing the opposite of what my competitors (and most other businesses) were doing. For my competitors, they would call and try to secure a job order for an open position within the client company. If the company didn't have any job openings (which was very common during the recession), they tried to convince them to see their sales rep for a face-to-face appointment, just in case a need arose. As you might imagine that strategy didn't work very well. I, on the other hand, *asked them* what the biggest staffing challenge was that they had. If they were seeking a rare "unicorn" employee, what did that person look like? Then, I went out and tried to find them. It worked. I was able to build relationships that bore fruit over the long-term—and to start placing high-margin workers even during the Great Recession.

Asking Questions During The COVID-19 Pandemic

A little over ten years after the Great Recession ended, I found myself in another period of economic contraction, this one caused by the COVID-19 pandemic. However, as you know by now, my coaching business ended up doubling between March 2020 and October 2020. But how?

It was actually pretty similar to the strategy I used with Diversified Industrial Staffing *during* the Great Recession. I had built a strong foundation for my coaching business. And I knew that my mission was to improve the lives of my clients and audiences by sharing the strategies I learned and used over the two decades I had been in business. That's important. My mission wasn't to make a bunch of money. Of course, building a profitable coaching business was important. I couldn't operate very long if my business were not profitable. But my mission was bigger than that; it was to share my strategies to improve lives. So that's what I did.

In this case, instead of calling on companies to find out what they wanted for labor, I reached out to people directly and on social media and asked them what they needed for help. When they told me, I coached them through their struggles for free. No questions asked. No strings attached. I gave dozens of entrepreneurs free help knowing I was getting zero payment and zero margin. They needed help, and it was my opportunity to be of service to CEOs and entrepreneurs wrapped up in chaos and crisis. As the economy rebounded, some of them reached out and hired me to help them on an ongoing basis. Others referred me to their friends or colleagues.

In the end, leaning into my mission and asking prospects what they needed for help led to me not only treading water throughout the recession but also doubling my business during COVID-19.

When times are tough, you can make more progress by asking questions and being helpful to your prospects than almost any other activity you can think of in business.

Leadership in the Trenches

As I was writing this book, I had the opportunity to attend the Virtual Agile Scaleup Summit 2.0, hosted by Verne Harnish, author of *Scaling Up*. Some of the best insights from speakers included the following:

- "Leaders absorb fear and exude hope."—Greg Brenneman
- "Resilience isn't bouncing back; it's bouncing forward."—Michael Bungay Stanier
- "Strategic distance, operational distance, and team distance are more perilous than physical distance."—Keith Ferrazzi

But when it comes to strategy, one of the true highlights was General Stanley McChrystal (Ret.), the bestselling author of *Team of Teams*, who spoke about what he called "Leadership in the Trenches." A retired four-star general who created counterinsurgency and counterterrorism strategies for the war in Afghanistan, McChrystal knows a thing or two about strategy.

During part of his leadership, he managed teams across twenty-seven countries and used video teleconferencing every day for ninety minutes with 7,500 people. Certainly, entrepreneurs adjusting to the "new normal" of work can relate to this. And perhaps all of us can relate to the feelings expressed by President Franklin D. Roosevelt in his famous 1933 inaugural speech, given right at the end of the Great Depression, which General McChrystal played at the Summit:

> I am certain that my fellow Americans expect that on my induction into the Presidency I will address them with a candor and a decision which the present situation of our people impels. This is preeminently the time to speak the truth, and boldly. Nor need we shrink from honestly facing conditions in our country today. This great Nation will endure as it has endured, will revive, and will prosper. So, first of all, let me assert my firm belief that the

only thing we have to fear is fear itself—nameless, unreasoning, unjustified terror which paralyzes needed efforts to convert retreat into advance. In every dark hour of our national life, a leadership of frankness and vigor has met with that understanding and support of the people themselves which is essential to victory. I am convinced that you will again give that support to leadership in these critical days.[67]

Perhaps surprisingly, General McChrystal's talk about "Leadership in the Trenches" didn't focus very much about strategy. It didn't focus on sophisticated maneuvers. It didn't focus on having the best product or service, or in his case the strongest military weapons and people. In the midst of the crisis, here's my summary of what McChrystal said to do:

We are in a crisis; what are we going to do about it? We can complain and feel sorry for ourselves. **We can quit. But that isn't what we want to do.**

Your strategy from earlier in the year isn't going to be the same going forward. Be honest with yourself and admit it. You probably don't know how to get from where you are now to where you want to be.

We are going to do what we need to do to win; **we are going to iterate as a team** *and figure out what works.*

We have to lead right now. *We need to be realistic and humble about how we do it.*

Start by being honest. Tell people the real situation. *Your team will fill the vacuum with the darkest of ideas. When things change, be honest with them again. You will be viewed as having integrity by being candid with them*

Be committed. *They need to know that you are in it now and will be in it the whole way through.*

Be present. *It might not be how you have done it in the past (walking around, etc.). Figure out how to be present virtually. You can't multitask. You need to intentionally communicate action steps* *through nonverbal communication.*

Ask questions *so that the person can show their expertise.*

Remember whom we are leading. *Many of your team members might have a lot of distractions around them. The fact that we work from home means that we also now never leave work. Team members might feel pressured and isolated.*

This is an opportunity to be better than we might have been and do more for others.

Above, I emphasized the points from General McChrystal that are at the core of the strategies in this book. Here are some examples of principles reflected along with one example from his talk:

Shifting Our Mind-Set
We can quit. But that isn't what we want to do.

ATV Leadership
Start by being honest. Tell people the real situation.

Setting Intentions, Not Expectations
You probably don't know how to get from where you are now to where you want to be.

The E-4 Process
Your strategy from earlier in the year isn't going to be the same going forward. Be honest with yourself and admit it. You probably don't know how to get from where you are now to where you want to be. We are going to do what we need to do to win; we are going to iterate as a team and figure out what works.

Looping toward Success
We have to lead right now. We need to be realistic and humble about how we do it.

Empowering Yourself with People

Remember whom we are leading. Many of your team members might have a lot of distractions around them. When we work from home, we never really leave work. Team members might feel pressured and isolated. This is an opportunity to be better than we might have been and do more for others.

I can't imagine a tougher challenge than managing thousands of military personnel around the world. We can't compare what we do in business to the challenges the military faces at home and abroad. But we can learn so much by listening to the great leaders when they're willing to share wisdom from the battlefield. And General McChrystal's advice confirms just how important it is to put in the work to build a solid foundation and then lean into your mission when times get tough.

Listen To Absorb, Not To Respond

As the leader of clients, team members, or even of our families and ourselves, our outcomes are often a direct result of our communication. That's even more important when times are tough. But we need to be even more intentional about how we communicate during times of crisis.

If you remember one rule of thumb when it comes to communication styles, it should be to "listen to absorb, not to respond." This is important in good times, of course. But it's even more important in bad times. When I called prospects about staffing needs during the Great Recession, I resisted the common urge to respond right away. Instead, I asked them what position or skill set they'd be most interested in hiring. They told me. I absorbed it, thanked them for their time, and used that information to pivot my business.

Way too many times, we listen to people's concerns and try to convince them that their concern is misplaced. When times are tough, do your best to avoid that temptation. When we listen to absorb, we're fully present and we can truly learn how to better lead the other person. It doesn't matter who it is—an upset client, a significant other planning a home improvement project, or a three-year-old refusing to eat their peas—you can do more good by absorbing what they say and not responding at all, than listening only to formulate a response. Look them in the eye if you're face-to-face.

Avoid scrolling through Instagram if you're on the phone. Be present. Be focused. And truly listen. Then ask yourself what they really want and practice the same creative thinking we talked about in Chapter 1.

The Frequency And Forms Of Effective Crisis Communication

When times are tough, the frequency and forms of communication we use can make a big difference in the effectiveness of our communications. For example, during the COVID-19 pandemic, I had a client who was communicating with her team on a daily basis while they were working from home. She sent out emails and gave updates about key business metrics. Her business had been hit hard, and most of her staff was laid off. She was trying to come up with ways to get people money. She emailed on a daily basis to let them know she was thinking of them, but nobody responded.

During a coaching call, I suggested she go in a different direction. Sending daily emails was a good idea, but long paragraphs of text couldn't adequately represent how hard she was working to support her team. I asked her to try sending a short video every morning. It didn't need to be anything highly produced. She could say the same exact thing that she'd say in email. But sending it as a video would allow her team to see her and hear her vocal inflection. She's a heart-centered leader and runs a heart-centered company. She really does care deeply for her people. Sending emails stripped the heart out of her message every morning, so we decided to try videos.

Every video started the same, with something to the effect of "Good morning. I'm thinking of you. I hope you and your family are well." It also included an invitation for them to reach out if they needed to talk about anything, such as, "If I can help you, please let me know. If you have any needs, I want to be here to help." She then updated her team in true ATV-leader style:

> Here's what I know about the company. Here's where we stand. I filled out an application for four government loans. The brutal reality is, I don't know when the money is going to come in, and I don't know if we're going to get the money if we do get the money.

If we do get approved for the money, I don't know how fast it will arrive in our bank account. Here's a plan I've got. I'm laying out a framework to do one, two, and three if we don't get the money. I'm also working on a contingency plan. Here's four, five, and six. Feel free to give me any feedback, please. Connect with me. I'm happy to chat with you at any time. Have a great day.

The entire video was less than two minutes long. The very first day, she went from receiving zero engagement to incredible engagement. It really landed with her people. So, when we think about communication, let's think about the frequency, but let's also think about the form, too. Are we heart centered? What is our vocal inflection? How do we care about others? How do we care about our team? How do we share what we don't know? How often should we communicate with that in mind? And what form of communication would most accurately reflect who we are?

Accountability, The Itty Bitty Shitty Committee, And Imposter Syndrome

Whether micro-crises or macro-crises, we will all face setbacks. It doesn't matter how strong our foundation or how well we lean into our mission and pivot, we will stumble. We'll lose clients. We'll lose money. We'll be scared. We'll eat a whole lot of humble pie. I don't want to give the impression that we can avoid disaster completely. We can't. We can limit the downside and accelerate our comeback, but we will face setbacks.

When that happens, we need to lean into three important concepts: personal accountability, what I call the "Itty Bitty Shitty Committee," and the Imposter Syndrome. Here's what you need to know about each of these so you can come out the other side stronger, straight from one of my most frustrating experiences of pulling myself out of debt.

Let's set the scene. I'm in the midst of getting myself out of $600,000 in debt. I have past-due receivables totaling hundreds of thousands of dollars. If my clients pay, it will make my life a whole lot easier. If not, I'll be in a world of hurt. One client owes my company more than $240,000. How did I let it get this bad?

I still have moments when I beat myself up about that moment in the past.

It happened. I shouldn't have extended them credit and crazy payment terms. I should have been on top of it. I held out hope for a while that they'd pay, but the day they filed for bankruptcy protection, all that hope was lost. When that happened, I asked myself what was wrong with me. Was I just bad at business? If so, I would be in big trouble because I was also a terrible employee. I couldn't imagine having to go back to working for someone else. I went on and on and on.

If that internal dialogue feels even somewhat familiar, you're likely already familiar with venturing into the territory of what I call the "Itty Bitty Shitty Committee." As entrepreneurs, we can jump from feeling invincible to feeling worthless in a matter of seconds. We think terrible things about ourselves and launch personal attacks on ourselves that are worse than we'd say to our worst enemy. Those "You're stupid. You're an idiot. What's wrong with you?" are moments that belong to the Itty Bitty Shitty Committee. You're being shitty to yourself and making yourself feel small.

But there's more. Sometimes, we stop there. We beat ourselves up a bit and snap out of it. Other times, we take it one step further. We tell ourselves that we don't have what it takes to ever succeed. And we often pair that "We'll never be able to do it" with a dose of paranoia, such as, "You're not good enough. Everybody knows. None of your team members is going to listen to you. Your clients will figure out that you're in way over your head. Everyone's going to find out that you're a fraud."

The day that client filed for bankruptcy protection, I called a *big* meeting of my Itty Bitty Shitty Committee and concluded that I was an Imposter. It happens a lot during times of crises. But it doesn't take a big mistake, or even a crisis, for us to call a meeting of our Itty Bitty Shitty Committee or struggle with Imposter Syndrome. It happens even in good times. So we need to be aware of it and how to respond in good times and in bad. And don't worry, I've yet to meet an entrepreneur who didn't have an Itty Bitty Shitty Committee or suffer from Imposter Syndrome. (Even the ones who present themselves as confident struggle with them. They just won't tell you, trust me.)

When we are active in business, we'll meet a lot of impressive people. And when that happens, we'll learn all about their résumés, business successes, and family highlights. When we do, we start comparing what they share with us to the realities of our lives that we experience on the inside. With social media, for example, we see people posting pictures of a fancy vacation and get jealous. It happens. We see it and start feeling like failures. But we don't know the full story. They don't post about their insecurities, only the highlights. Yet that doesn't make it any less likely that we'll start beating ourselves up or feeling like a failure.

In business, it happens frequently, too. With me, I might go to a trade show, or a networking event, or the Gathering of Titans meeting at MIT. I show up and look around the room and think, "Everybody's smarter than I am. Everybody's better than I am. Everybody's more successful than I am." It happens almost every time, even though I'm highly aware of it. If I don't catch myself, those voices of self-doubt become crippling.

> "I was gauging my actions and the success of my actions on the end result. I had to reframe that to say, 'Look, your success needs to be looked at and predicated on the steps that get to that end result.' I was being hard on myself because I wasn't getting the end result. I was becoming completely stuck, unable to take action. So I needed to be conscientious of the steps I was taking and breaking it down into smaller pieces and just work the plan."
> — Eric Samdahl, COO, The HT Group, on his personal Itty Bitty Shitty Committee

So what do we do when we call a meeting of the Itty Bitty Shitty Committee or struggle with Imposter Syndrome? The first thing we need to do is to have awareness and recognize it's there. The second thing we need to do is slow down and take a deep breath and approach our Itty Bitty Shitty Committee with massive curiosity—question it, ask it what it's doing in our head at this time. Emotions build like snowballs. The longer we let them move on their own, the bigger and stronger they'll get and the harder they'll be to stop. By dealing with our reactivity, it will slow down and begin to defuse.

Once we feel that negative energy slow down, we need to immediately pivot to the E-4 Process. Identify what's not working. In this case, making assumptions about other people and ourselves isn't working. The narrative we are telling ourselves also isn't working. Next, set a new intention. What are we really looking to achieve? With that $240,000 bankruptcy, I was looking to keep my business afloat and build stronger financials. Next, we need to get help, plan, and pivot. One helpful way to end a meeting of an Itty Bitty Shitty Committee is to invite someone you trust into the room to help you shift your focus. In a trade show, for example, you could strike up a conversation with a vendor or someone you know. In your daily life, you could call a confidant, coach, or friend. (Greg and Dr. Friedland have received many calls from me in the midst of a meeting of my Itty Bitty Shitty Committee over the years.) Finally, iterate and repeat. Once you break the cycle, focus your energy on the next best step to achieve your intention. Often, this involves working to remain in creative thinking mode about achieving what's truly important in both the moment and the big picture.

Suck vs. Success

I've envisioned the Itty Bitty Shitty Committee as a dark passenger sitting next to me in my car. I'm driving down the highway, and before I realize it, I'm in the passenger seat and the dark passenger is behind the wheel. I'm no longer in control. I'm going wherever he takes me. I'm heading toward a world of suck.

But once I become aware of it, I can deal with it. But I need to get back in the driver's seat and grab hold of the wheel. He might still be there, but I get back in the driver's seat, the Itty Bitty Shitty Committee is back in the passenger seat, and I'm back steering the car toward success.

Imposter Syndrome and the Itty Bitty Shitty Committee isn't all bad, though. My coach Dr. Friedland, who I mentioned earlier, once told me that both the Itty Bitty Shitty Committee and Imposter Syndrome might help us out at times. If we're aware of it, we can treat it like we would a conversation with an upset customer or team member.

In that case, we can apply the "listen to absorb" lessons we talked about earlier and learn something valuable about ourselves. We can shift the negative self-talk into something more productive. And that can prevent us from making decisions that would be counterproductive. In the past, it could have prevented us from heading closer to a world of suck, too, even if we didn't know it. But for today, our primary goal is to recognize it's there and be ready to shift to the E-4 Process to help break the momentum.

The E-4 Process In Action

During the initial impact of COVID-19, I cohosted a webinar with brand expert Deb Gabor called "Banish the Itty Bitty Shitty Committee in Your Head: E-4 Process to Achieving a Growth Mind-Set."

During that session, Gabor and I discussed how many Itty Bitty Shitty Committees had been called to order. Entrepreneurs all around the world were scared, frustrated, and beating themselves up as they tried to navigate the unknown.

Gabor then shared her own tale with listeners:

> It was a huge pitch pivot for me. I make most of my money from speaking engagements and doing workshops and things like that. When all of that revenue went away, you know, I had that moment where I had my Itty Bitty Shitty Committee in my head. It was a huge pity party that I was throwing for myself, but I quickly swung into action.

Action is the only way to disband your Itty Bitty Shitty Committee or move past Imposter Syndrome. When it happens to you, use the E-4 Process and get to work.

Accepting Feedback After Action, Even During Stressful Times

Feedback is inevitable in anything you do, regardless of whether the strategy around our intention works. And feedback can come from multiple sources: clients, employees, shareholders, and family. During any time, the best leaders accept feedback and use it to iterate and pivot their way along the looping line of success. During tough times, however, accepting feedback is even more important.

Tough times in our companies are defined by uncertainty, high emotions, and elevated stress levels. Decisions are made with limited information. If we were being completely blunt, our answer to pretty much every question would be "I don't know." But we can't just sit back and wait to have complete clarity before making decisions. We need to move forward and make the best decisions possible with the information we have. How? Use the E-4 Process: identify what's not working; set an intention; get help, plan, and pivot; and iterate and repeat.

There it is. Get help—especially during tough times when you are moving forward with limited information. That help—the feedback—can come from several places: family, friends, team members, or even outside coaches and consultants. When I offered free coaching to people during the COVID-19 pandemic, that's exactly what the people who took me up on my offer did.

Getting feedback helps by taking out some of the emotions from the decision tree, especially when the feedback comes from people outside of your business. And remember, feedback from team members and customers gives you valuable information from people directly involved in buying, selling, and delivering your products and services to customers. In the end, you make better, more informed, and less emotional decisions. That said, knowing how important it is to accept feedback doesn't make it much easier to do. That takes practice. It takes removing pride and ego from the feedback equation. Over time, it will become easier if we practice receiving and evaluating feedback to help us make better decisions.

Evaluating feedback needs to come from a place of massive curiosity. We need to look at what's being said, what's not being said, who is giving us the feedback, and what it all means. For example, instead of writing off feedback from a team member who is a frequent complainer, we can ask ourselves the following: What is the stated meaning? What is the unstated meaning? What is the stated intention? What is the unstated intention? And finally, where within the feedback is the useful learning opportunity?

Take a look at my friend Andy Buyting, who owns a multimedia publishing company called Tulip Media Group. Andy is a master of receiving and using feedback to iterate and improve his business. In fact, he lives by the philosophy, "Don't sacrifice great to keep something that's mediocre." Like my mission to help entrepreneurs by sharing my decades of business experience helped guide me during the COVID-19 pandemic, Andy's philosophy of constantly pushing for greatness has guided him for years.

For example, when Andy started Tulip Media Group, he observed that his salespeople were never hitting their sales goals. Never. In many businesses, the leader would have tried to find better salespeople or redesign his offers (with so many salespeople failing, it was possible that the offer wasn't good enough). Not Andy. He leaned on partners, staff, and others for advice. In the end, he realized his offer was fine. The problem was his sales process didn't match his intention of getting his publishing services in front of ideal customers. More of his ideal customers were shopping for his offerings online.

With that information in mind, Andy took bold, swift, and decisive action, firing all of his salespeople and pivoting to a new sales strategy. After firing his salespeople, he held a companywide meeting to explain that the direction of the company wouldn't change but the sales strategy would pivot toward pay-per-click and online marketing.

Andy told me he was thinking, "Well, I'm taking a big risk, but I'm also taking the big risk off the table based on the feedback I've received, because what we had been doing wasn't working." As a leader, he leaned into those uncomfortable decisions, got help, created a plan, and took action. And it all started with the realization that what he had been doing wasn't working. Within six weeks of his new sales strategies, his company hit the sales objectives for the first time ever. The next quarter, they tripled the objective and hit it again. They even hit their sales objectives during the COVID-19 pandemic.

Andy's example makes an important point. When he fired his sales team, he wasn't in the midst of a macro-crisis, like the COVID-19 pandemic; he was in the midst of a micro-crisis, with his salespeople failing to support the company's operations. When multiple salespeople consistently fail to hit targets, it would have been easy for someone in Andy's position to change offerings, reduce pricing, or even shut down the business because not enough people were buying. But Andy didn't do that. He got feedback. And that feedback told him that neither his offerings nor the specific salespeople were the problem. It told him that the entire sales process was the problem. So he shifted that, and the rest is history.

Laying Your Foundation And Staying the Course

Remember my opening story of getting life-changing advice from my brother and coach, Greg, in 2006? He led me through a massive shift from the negative to the positive, which set me up much better for handling the Great Recession in the late 2000s. When the recession hit, staying the course and leaning on the E-4 Process helped me come out of the recession stronger than ever. As Greg recently observed,

> Todd was doing large contracts and competing against billion-dollar companies. But after digging into the data, we realized he could make more money by doing more niche staffing. For the time being, he could still service his existing accounts, provided that he changed some of his policies, most notably reducing his accounts receivable timeline. He still had those relationships and could make those accounts work in the short term until he got enough high-margin contracts in place. As he secured more contacts, he realized that the world of high-margin specialized staffing was one with much less competition.

> Todd's pivot worked so well because he worked very intentionally toward a better future. He first identified what wasn't working. In his case, he was bleeding cash and operating with razor-thin margins. He set the intention of paying down his debt and then got help, made a plan to improve cash flow and margins, and then took action. As he received feedback from the market, he iterated and repeated. But in the end, he became known as an expert in a niche labor category and built a bigger, stronger company that helped him navigate good times and bad.

If you are in the midst of a crisis and haven't yet laid a strong foundation, start now. I helped many entrepreneurs navigate the COVID-19 pandemic who hadn't yet built a strong foundation. It's more challenging but not impossible. Just lean into the strategies and the E-4 Process. Practice creative thinking. Set new intentions. Observe ATV leadership. Get help, plan, and pivot. Take action, iterate, and repeat. If you're committed, you can do it.

But if you *have* built the foundation, it will make it much easier for you to navigate tough times. I've helped countless coaching clients navigate micro-crises and the inevitable recessions that pop up every ten years or so by building businesses that worked in good times and in bad. And I have done it myself with my companies. The formula isn't complicated:

- Set a solid foundation.
- Set a vision.
- Set a positive mind-set.
- Set yourself up for opportunities.
- Keep going, following the E-4 Process all along the way.
- Keep your focus.
- Keep curious.
- Stay the course.

During tough times, being able to rely on a proven system to strengthen and endure can make or break your future. The strategies in this book and staying the course during micro- or macro-crises can set you up for success and help you avoid a world of suck. Lean into what works and know that you don't need to do it alone. Extraordinary entrepreneurs always get feedback.

In the next chapter, we're going to take extraordinary entrepreneurship to a whole new level to help you not only build a business that serves you well but also a life you may have only dreamed of living.

Insights

- Leadership is universal. It shows up in family, in business, in the military, and everywhere else.
- Listen to absorb, not respond.
- Decisions need to be made with all available information. You will never have 100 percent of the information, so make the best decision you can with what you have. Then pivot to a new decision based on the new information.

Questions For Reflection

- What message am I receiving from my Itty Bitty Shitty Committee?
- What results are showing up in my life from the messages I receive from my Itty Bitty Shitty Committee?
- How can I improve my communication skills?

Action Steps

- Practice active listening all day, every day.
- Get comfortable with feedback. Welcome it into your world.

Additional Resources

McChrystal, (Ret.) Gen. Stanley. *Team of Teams: New Rules of Engagement for a Complex World.* New York: Portfolio / Penguin, 2015.

Also visit ExtraordinaryAdvisors.com for more exclusive coaching tips.

Chapter 8

Designing Your
Ultimate Life

*"Dysfunctional belief: If you are successful, you will be happy. Reframe: True happiness comes
from designing a life that works for you."*
— Coauthor/Stanford Professor Bill Burnett, Designing Your Life:
How to Build a Well-Lived, Joyful Life

For nearly forty years, Nigel Bennett has been one of Canada's top environmental consultants and one of the world's top manufacturers of oil-spill-response equipment, having founded Aqua-Guard Spill Response. For decades, he built his reputation and a business to support it. From the outside, you'd think he was living his dream life. Behind the scenes, however, his business and life were both chaotic.

In 2012, with a small business starting to grow, Bennett had everything leveraged. "I was living in complete chaos," he says. "I call it the doorknob effect. Every day, I'd come to the office and I'd touch the doorknob, and I'd step into chaos. In the shower, I'd think, 'Do I have to lay people off today, or can I hire people today? Can I make payroll today?'"

In the midst of that chaos, a friend of his told him about a group called the Young Entrepreneurs' Organization, or YEO, (now called Entrepreneurs' Organization, or EO). His friend was pretty well connected and a professional football player in the Canadian Football League. Nigel trusted him completely. On the advice his friend, Nigel joined YEO and started working with a leadership coach.

When he started attending YEO meetings, Nigel assumed he would be surrounded by business leaders who had everything together. To his surprise, he realized the opposite, that he was not alone in his woes. "I thought I was the only one on the planet living like this," he says. "When I sat with these people, I realized that we're all the same."

Working with a coach was really tough at first, Nigel says. "As an entrepreneur, I was never really accountable to anybody other than my wife and kids," he says. "But having a coach made me truly accountable for the first time." That discomfort led to him realizing how helpful having built-in accountability was for his business (and mental) health.

Taking the uncomfortable steps of joining YEO and working with a coach led to Nigel becoming even more aggressive in his search for a better business and personal life. He learned lessons from everywhere he went and everyone he encountered. Life was finally on the upswing.

Unfortunately, the more he learned, the more he felt that he hadn't found his life's purpose yet. But he didn't lose hope. He continued to learn. Eventually, he ended up as a classmate of mine at the Gathering of Titans at MIT. His journey as a lifelong learner took him on a trip to the Amazon rainforest, where he reached a breakthrough that would impact both his business and personal life for years to come.

"I was really fumbling around, trying to understand what my life's purpose was for many, many years," he says. "I'm still not 100 percent clear, but I know I'm going in the right direction."

That last sentence is important. So many people feel the need to become 100 percent clear on their purpose before pursuing a better life. When Nigel conceded that he was not 100 percent clear but knew he was heading in the right direction, it told me everything I needed to know about Nigel's pursuit for life's purpose. It told me he is instinctively working the E-4 Process toward a better, more meaningful life. He set an intention, was getting help, and was moving forward with a commitment to iterating and pivoting. There's no doubt that will lead him toward his dream life.

It might not take a trip to the Amazon to help you completely shift your perspective like it did for Nigel, but you can learn from Nigel's story. Read more about Nigel and his journey in his book, *Take That Leap: Risking It All for What Really Matters.*

The same principles that help us lead a strong business can help lead us to a greater purpose in our personal lives, too. And isn't that what's most important? What good is having a strong business if we don't live a life of purpose and passion? Yes, there will be seasons during which we need to focus more attention on our business and make sacrifices in our personal lives. But if that's the norm with no end in sight, design the life you want and build your business to support it. Only then will you truly enjoy your business and make an impact on the world that makes you proud.

Life By Design

In 2016, Stanford's Bill Burnett and Dave Evans published the book, *Designing Your Life: How to Build a Well-Lived, Joyful Life*. The book introduced the world to the concept of design thinking—basically how designers build their way forward instead of letting the Itty Bitty Shitty Committee constantly drag them down. I recently had the opportunity to talk with one of their disciples, Eugene Korsunskiy, an assistant professor at Dartmouth University who specializes in human-centered design. I asked Eugene to talk to entrepreneurs about design thinking and how it can be used to build not only a business you love but also a truly joyful life. As Eugene explains, design thinking involves using mind-sets and tools. "Together, they are a really helpful framework from which to guide creative action," he says. From a mind-set perspective, this involves taking on cognitive dispositions such as embracing experimentation, curiosity, optimism, empathy, and collaborating across differences. From a tools perspective, design thinking involves using research and ideation to constantly improve.

Design thinking works well because it helps avoid letting problems derail you. Instead, you move forward with empathy and an iterative mind. Design thinkers research the people involved with their goal in mind and design solutions that help everyone.

"When faced with an open-ended problem, the very first thing a designer does is build empathy for the people they're designing for," Eugene says. "If they're designing a medical device for doctors, they'll spend hours upon hours of their life in hospitals, talking to doctors, talking to patients, in order to learn as much as they can about the topic."

Design thinking for entrepreneurs looking to build a life of greater purpose and passion involves taking the same approach for your business or personal life. "When you are the person you're designing for, when it's your life or professional career or relationships, the number one most important thing to do at the beginning is to build empathy for yourself," Eugene says. "Most people think they know themselves, and most people don't know themselves as well as they need to or want to, which is why designers advocate reflection and journaling and paying attention to how you think and how you feel—what makes you tick and what your interests are and what your curiosities are—in order to really understand. What kinds of things give you energy; what kinds of things give you joy?"

If those steps look familiar, it's because they're very similar to the first steps of the E-4 Process, only applied to personal desires. We identify what's not working and set an intention for the life we want to live.

> "Every artist has thousands of bad drawings in them, and the only way to get rid of them is to draw them out."
> — Chuck Jones, Academy-Award-winning animated filmmaker and cartoonist of such classics as Looney Tunes and the animated movie, *How the Grinch Stole Christmas!*

The next step, explains Eugene, is turning these realizations into proactive ideas. Which ones are the most important? Which ones are the most problematic? "When you're working on your career or business," he says, "it's important to pause and think, 'OK, of all the things I have reflected and know about myself, which ones are the ones that are pointing me in the direction of joy and exploration?' Then comes one of the most fun parts of the design-thinking process, which is coming up with ideas. In brainstorming an idea, designers lower their inhibition. They stretch their imagination. They allow themselves to consider options that are silly or impractical: 'Let's just throw Post-its on the walls.'"

Life by design is essentially what I'm trying to create for myself and my life, my business, my family. *What is it that I want? What is the design that I want to create for myself?* You know, it's more than just me. It's more than just doing what I want, when I want. *What does it mean? How do I define it? How do I learn more about myself?* We have to be willing to be vulnerable—be willing to peel back the layers. Yes. And if you are willing and ready and able to go into it with full honesty and vulnerability with yourself, you will reap the greatest reward. Wait until you're ready, because life is going to throw a lot of curveballs at you, and this process is going to throw a lot of curveballs at you. You're going to find things about yourself that you never realized or something that you just don't like. And you have to be ready to take that on.

— Jessica Moseley, CEO, iYellow Group, and client

"Psychological research," says Eugene, "suggests that if you allow yourself and your brain to go to a place that's a little bit off the beaten path, a little bit impractical, a little bit weird, a little bit wacky, then you are way more likely to bring back from that place, back to reality, some idea that is novel, interesting, creative, innovative, and one that you wouldn't have been able to have before."

Using Stress As A Sign

Even the most detailed and successful design thinking can't stop the looping line of success from sending us backwards, though. The loops will happen. We can help flatten it somewhat, but we can't avoid it completely. And we can better prepare for it to come out of the chaos better, but we can't keep all chaos at bay. (I've certainly felt it myself writing this book!)

The only way we can succeed in our businesses and personal lives is by pushing ourselves a bit beyond our comfort zones. We need to be willing to get uncomfortable in the present to build more strength and comfort for the future. When we do, we'll realize discomfort is actually a good thing because it allows for incredible breakthroughs. While this is hard to do in business, it's even harder for entrepreneurs to do so in their personal lives. That's because entrepreneurs often have less autonomy and clarity in their personal lives. Many also struggle with damaged relationships, so it takes a lot more effort to build trust with spouses, kids, and other key people in our personal lives.

For those reasons and more, our stress levels often rise even greater when we start working toward a greater personal life. Because stress will be high, it's important that we put the stress in perspective to keep it from stopping us. Stress is neither good nor bad. Specifically, like I described in Chapter 1 when I encouraged you to use discomfort as a sign to take action, stress can be used the same way.

My coach and mentor, Daniel Friedland, who we discussed earlier in the book, explains it best in his book, *Leading Well from Within: A Neuroscience and Mindfulness-Based Framework for Conscious Leadership*:

> As you engage with what matters most to you and challenge the limits of your capability, you can expect to experience healthy levels of stress (or eustress). This kind of stress is what fuels your best performance and allows you to experience that sense of flow and well-being at the peak of your performance cure.

> In *The Upside of Stress*, Kelly McGonigal highlights a surprising finding from a study of the 2005–2006 Gallup World Poll. The Gallup researchers asked more than 125,000 people from 121 countries to indicate whether they had experienced a significant amount of stress in the previous day in order to calculate each nation's stress index. The study found that the higher the nation's stress index, the higher the nation's well-being. Further, individuals who were stressed but not depressed, i.e., amped-up and positively activated by their stress, experienced higher life satisfaction. This study suggests that stress, when leveraged as an asset to engage with what you most care about, goes hand in hand with well-being, meaning, and fulfillment.

> Still, the process of creating your ideal life design can feel daunting. You may feel overwhelmed, unsure where to begin. Or you may be experiencing a fear of failure (or even a fear of success), which can lead to avoidance and procrastination and ultimately cause you to slip down the right side of the stress and performance curve.

If you do find yourself slipping down the right side of the curve into distress, try reappraising this entire process as the enlivening adventure of a lifetime and then break the process down into a framework with bite-sized, easy-to-implement steps.[68]

If you let stress stop you, you will continue to live a life far below what's possible. If you instead use it as a sign to use the E-4 Process to set and pursue a new intention, the sky's the limit on the impact and fulfillment you can achieve. Use stress as a sign that you're heading toward something better, and use the E-4 Process to keep you moving forward.

The Power Of Perspective When Pursuing A Better Personal Life

No matter how strong your business becomes, if it's not built to help you achieve the personal life you desire, you will never feel truly fulfilled. You must tap into your deep desires on a personal level and build your business to support that vision. Otherwise, you might end up building a company you hate because it quite literally keeps you from the life you want. You'll resent it. And the more successful it becomes, the more stressful you'll become because it will be an even bigger and stronger barrier to the life you want to live.

Unfortunately, we often lack perspective even more in our personal lives than we do in our businesses. Entrepreneurs spend more time in their businesses. They have more data in their businesses. They get feedback from more people in their businesses.

That's why it's so important to get help when designing your life. It's never work/life balance as an entrepreneur. It's work/life integration to fully create your life by design. If you're working with a coach, make sure you are creating a holistic plan to build a business that supports the personal life you desire. Make sure your coach helps you get feedback and perspective in your personal life. Be as intentional about your personal intentions as you are with your business intentions. It's the only way for an entrepreneur to build a truly successful business.

If you're not working with a coach, maybe you have a friend or trusted colleague who can help you get started. You will still need to filter their feedback like you would any other feedback. Filter their feedback to identify intentions or biases. Approach their well-intended feedback with massive curiosity, to best get to the root of their feedback. Then put together a plan, take action, and iterate.

Of course, I'm biased. I highly recommend involving a truly neutral observer whose job is solely focused on helping you achieve extraordinary results. That's why I'm so passionate about coaching and encourage people to invest in hiring a coach who can help them succeed. Like any important asset, you're worth investing in yourself, and the future you want to build is worth taking seriously. And just like Tom Schwab, who built a highly profitable company before hiring me as a coach and then increasing profits by 500 percent in the first year, the benefits you can experience when you invest in yourself can be surprising. That's why I am always working with at least one coach.

Shifting your perspective, laying out a life by design, and working with a coach can be your roadmap to the life you want to create, too.

Insights

- Empathy is a key component of creating a life by design.
- Stress is an asset when properly leveraged. It is neither good nor bad.
- Work/life balance is a myth. For entrepreneurs, it's work/life integration.

Questions For Reflection

- Do I need to hire a coach to help me create my life by design or help me deal with the chaos in my business?
- Where in my life am I dissatisfied? Can I apply design thinking to solve this issue?

Action Steps

- Invest in your most valuable asset: yourself.

Additional Resources

Bennett, Nigel. *Take That Leap: Risking It All for What Really Matters.* 614929 B.C. Ltd., 2018.

Burnett, Bill, and Dave Evans. *Designing Your Life: Build a Life That Works for You.* London: Chatto & Windus, 2013.

Friedland, Daniel. *Leading Well from Within: A Neuroscience and Mindfulness-Based Framework for Conscious Leadership.* San Diego: SuperSmartHealth, 2016.

McGonigal, Kelly. *The Upside of Stress: Why Stress Is Good for You, and How to Get Good at It.* New York: Avery, 2015.

Also visit ExtraordinaryAdvisors.com for more exclusive coaching tips.

Conclusion And Next Steps

"An entrepreneur alone is an entrepreneur at risk."—*Anonymous*

If you've read this far, there is one thing I know for sure. Information is not your greatest obstacle to avoiding a world of suck and moving more confidently toward success.

I knew that before you even started reading, however. While you might not have had a simplified E-4 Process at your fingertips, you likely had more than enough information to build a better business and personal life.

But I know that information alone doesn't change your life. It's what you do with that information that will change your life. So, instead of ending the book with just a summary of information, I want to leave you with some questions and action steps as well, along with an invitation to reach out to me if you're struggling. Like I did during the macro-crisis all businesses experienced during the COVID-19 pandemic, I invite you to a free, no-pressure call to help you navigate whatever troubled waters you're experiencing right now. Just email me at todd@extraordinaryadvisors.com and mention this book. You invested your time reading the strategies I shared here. I'm happy to invest my time on a call to help you start applying them.

As you begin to apply these strategies in your life, I encourage you to avoid one of the biggest obstacles to progress: going at it alone. I'm obviously biased as a coach, but I've seen it happen over and over again, so let me share the three biggest pieces of value people experience when getting help. I'll use coaching as an example because that's where most of my experience is, both as a coach and as a coaching client. If you can get these benefits in other ways, I encourage you to do so, because, without a doubt, you will achieve much greater progress and have a much easier time when you move forward with the right help than you will trying to go at it alone.

Greater Vision

Getting help will give you greater vision in your business and personal life. As a coach, I come to every call with a unique advantage. I can see things that my clients cannot.

I'm not stuck in the day-to-day drama of running a business like my clients are. I'm not putting out fires. I'm not emotionally connected to their staff or customers. And I don't carry years of disappointment or emotional stress that can cloud them in their personal lives.

I also come with decades of experience and institutional knowledge. I have learned from my own experience as well as from working with hundreds of people just like them. I am a lifelong learner. I still use a coach myself. I can see more and help more with every passing day.

Together, that experience helps me support my clients with greater objectivity and expertise than they would achieve by going at it alone. They leave our call better prepared and with more confidence to move forward. If you only want to benefit from your own experience, rolling up your sleeves, staying late, and working harder and harder is the plan. But your ceiling will be lower, and your life will be harder.

If you want to benefit from other people's vision and experience, getting help from someone with collective experience from hundreds of other businesses can help you work smarter, not just harder, and achieve a higher ceiling in a shorter period of time.

More Confidence

Getting help will boost your confidence as you navigate uncertainty and fight the Imposter Syndrome and Itty Bitty Shitty Committee. This is especially important because it's not a matter of if you experience uncertainty, Imposter Syndrome, and a meeting of the Itty Bitty Shitty Committee, it's when. When it happens, your results will be a direct consequence of the decisions you make and actions you take.

As a coach, I can't even count how many times a client entered a call overwhelmed and unsure of themselves. This doesn't just happen when navigating a crisis, either. In fact, more frequently, clients experience confidence challenges because they're working on taking their business or personal lives to new heights. They are trying to achieve different results, so they're taking different actions than they have in the past.

Achieving different results and taking different actions often naturally leads to fluctuating levels of confidence. As an experienced and objective observer, I've seen others achieve similar goals and helped them do so. I know what it takes. And I know what they've done to prepare. So I also know they have what it takes to achieve the results they want and can help them move forward.

My objectivity and perspective helps me believe in my clients when they cannot believe in themselves. It helps me see the potential in them while they struggle to put their mistakes and insecurities in the rear view mirror. And it allows them to plug into their feelings of being "less than" and let them plug into my confidence in their infinite abundance and infinite possibilities. They leave the call more confident and prepared to move forward.

Higher Levels Of Success

Getting help lets people aim higher and find higher levels of success. An experienced and objective coach will push you to a higher level than you ever thought possible on your own.

The art of coaching, I've learned, is not just performing active coaching, it's also teaching self-coaching to clients so they can continue to benefit between calls. That means they are better prepared for achieving higher long-term results.

Coaches will call you out when you're aiming too low. They will push you forward when you're struggling. And they will hold you accountable for doing the work you agreed to do.

An Extraordinary Life

By reading this book, you have already proven you are not ordinary. You are not mundane, or run-of-the-mill, or average.

Are you extraordinary? Only you can determine that. But I'll bet you feel a few steps closer to singular and special. You've learned how to define your own success. You now have an iterative attitude to cope with failure. And you're beginning to realize self-actualization.

Together, we have reclaimed the world extraordinary.

Questions For Reflection

As we finish our time together, I'll leave you with two things. First, I'll give you a list of questions I would ask of a new coaching client to help them achieve clarity and direction as they begin a new path to avoiding a world of suck and pursuing extraordinary success. I'll do that in this section to get you thinking about yourself and your future in a way that positions you to succeed. Then, I'll leave you with a lesson about failure that I learned from a nine-year-old boy named Alec.

Here are the questions I want you to reflect on today:

- What is the #1 negative belief you have that is holding you back from attaining your life by design?
- What is your Itty Bitty Shitty Committee telling you? What do you believe about yourself that is holding you back from building a better business and life?
- Where do you struggle with Imposter Syndrome? Are those insecurities based in reality, or are you just being too hard on yourself? Challenge yourself to take a more objective approach to your capabilities.
- What expectations are you currently holding onto—whether it's family, business, or personal—that you can move away from and replace with intentions?

If you need help answering those questions, please take me up on my offer to invest in a phone call in helping you. Just email me at todd@extraordinaryadvisors.com and mention this book to set up a call.

Now, what can we learn about failure from a nine-year-old? Alec approached me after a talk I gave in Toronto several years ago. Like most of my talks, I had spoken about how great a teacher failure can be and encouraged the audience to embrace it when it happens. When Alec got to the front of the room, he handed me a diagram he drew. This is what the diagram looked like.

Thirteen boxes, twelve with the letter F—for failing—in them, and only one box with the letter S—for success—in it. As I looked at the paper, I immediately recognized F as the shorthand for failure that grade school kids are used to from report card grading. I looked back up from the page and made eye contact with Alec. Before I could say a thing, Alec smiled and said, "It doesn't matter how many times you fail, right? All you need is one success."

Alec taught me a lesson that day that I continue to think about to this day. Business and life isn't about avoiding failure. It's about still moving forward and pursuing success despite past failures. We don't need more successes than failures to lead a great life. We only need one. When we are pursuing a business and life of our own design, just one success will bring us more joy and fulfillment than we ever dreamed possible.

A nine-year-old boy taught me that lesson.

And I want the same for you. I don't care how many boxes you could draw with a big letter F in them. You can't go back in time and change those grades, so stop lamenting about what happened in the past. Instead, take out a piece of paper and draw one more box. Leave it empty for now. Then get to work, and you, too, can achieve more success than you ever thought possible. And when you're ready to write that S in there, shoot me an email so I can celebrate with you.

So what will it be?

Are you going to be limited by fear and self-doubt? Are you going to let expectations of yourself and others continue to disappoint you? Continue to hold you back? Or are you going to take control of your future and achieve the success and fulfillment you so deeply desire?

I challenge all of you to step up to your launchpad and adopt the lessons from this book. Take something from the stories you've heard throughout the book—the Nigel Bennetts, the Tom Schwabs, the Jacki Smiths, the Barbara Corcorans. If they can build businesses and personal lives of their dreams, there's no reason you can't—but you need to take action.

And if you want help and direction, reach out to me at todd@ extraordinaryadvisors.com today. Let's schedule thirty minutes to help you become a success story that inspires another entrepreneur like you to take action in the future.

Acknowledgments

I am grateful to all the wonderful people who have come into my life. So many of you have impacted me, challenged me, shifted my thoughts and my heart. Writing this book has been a start-and-stop journey for nearly five years. The contributions that show up throughout the book have been accumulated over a lifetime.

Each of the people recognized here have profoundly impacted me in my life, my successes, my mission. Without them being a part of my life's journey, this book would not exist. The gift of your presence runs through the text of this book.

To my brother and first coach, Greg Palmer. Simply put—this book would not exist if not for your guidance, love, and support. I have no doubts that much of my success in turning around Diversified Industrial Staffing is owed to your advice and input. You always picked up the phone when I called. In my darkest days, I could count on you to not let me fail. Your legacy of impact is carried forward with every leader that I now coach. I love you.

To Tyler Palmer, my son. Being your dad has been the biggest blessing of my life. Being a single parent has been the most rewarding job of my life. I know that my life as an entrepreneur and CEO wasn't always easy on you, and I appreciate your patience with me. I'm proud of the man you've become! I love you.

To Beverly Palmer. Well, Mom, I did it . . . from the days of writing for the school newspaper to my second book. I always appreciated your unwavering faith (regardless of my missteps, LOL). Wish you could be here to see this. Love you.

To Jen and Etta Jane Bartes, the two ladies of my life. You have challenged me to grow beyond my sometimes-rigid mind-set, and you have allowed me the privilege of impacting your lives. Etta Jane, you are the embodiment of infinite possibility. You are supercurious about the world, you have keen insights into others' feelings and emotions, and you are wise beyond your years. Jen, you are the passionate love of my life. You and your gypsy soul bring carefree joy to my life. Your willingness to struggle and never stop growing is refreshing. Your selfless kindness towards others—and animals—is something I continue to learn from.

To my EO Detroit Forum—Brian Dietz, David Petoskey, Scott Rice, Kevin Harman, Royce Neubauer, Pat Fehring, and Scott Eisenberg. I've learned and grown so much as a coach and teammate of our forum, I cannot thank you all enough for your willingness to share your vulnerability, wisdom, time, and insights with me over many years.

To Scott Rice, my favorite over-40-year-old basketball player. Your levelheaded, pragmatic contributions are very appreciated in my life. I can count on you to approach any issue with curiosity, to help create clarity. You have a keen ability to slow things down and help me think clearly when I am in my most-heightened state. Thank you for helping me create awareness in my life and for telling me what I needed to hear, not always what I wanted to hear.

To Scott Jackson. You are my brother from another mother. You are one of the few people I'd want to share a foxhole with. You are someone who is nonjudgmental and someone whom I can share my authentic self with. As a fellow single dad, I admire your success as both an entrepreneur and as Lilly's dad.

To Joe Bastian. My inspiring friend, who pushes me to see myself beyond my self-imposed limits. I appreciate you always pushing me to be the best thought leader I can be. Often, you see my blind spots and shed light onto them. I appreciate your never-ending rallying around my cause to improve lives.

To Tom Schwab. Thank you for challenging me to get this book written sooner rather than later. Your willingness to challenge my thinking around this project is much appreciated. You are a great man, an awesome client, and a trusted friend.

To Pattie Shefferly and Jim Lilly—two of the most trustworthy people I've ever met. The financial guidance you've provided personally and professionally through S and S Bookkeeping has been life changing. The kindness and friendship you exhibited in my darkest days will never be forgotten.

To the Diversified Industrial Staffing Team. This story would never have happened without your creativity, hard work, candidate-centric beliefs, and teamwork. A special thank you to Becky Lawson, Lisa Crawford, and Jeremy Dewald for your tireless contributions.

To my Extraordinary Advisors Clients. Being your coach is the professional joy of my life. Thank you for your trust in me. Your willingness to show up, do the hard work, and create the transformations each of you have made as leaders is inspiring!

To the other two of the three CEOs: Andy Buyting and Nigel Bennett. I have learned so much from both of you regarding generosity, servant leadership, giving back to others, and about focusing on what really matters. You are both survivors. It's an honor to be a member of our trio. Maybe one day we will write a book together!

To Sarah Tuff Dunn, Mary Meldrum, and John S. Schultz. Thank you all for helping me write this book. It was a winding journey, filled with stops and starts. I appreciate your patience and insights and taking on the task of being the critical eye of the reader. This book is better because of you.

To Mark Harris, my college department head. You were the first person to share with me that life was meant to be lived and college classes should be taken for the learning opportunities, not just grades. The many generous lunches that we shared, where you listened to my angst and uncertainty as an undergrad, were excellent role modeling of servant leadership I still reflect upon often.

Epilogue

The Foreword to this book was written by my good friend and longtime coach, Dr. Daniel Friedland.

The end of this book is a heartfelt tribute to Dr. Daniel Friedland.

As I was preparing to send *From Suck to Success,* I learned that Dr. Friedland had just been diagnosed with (Grade 4 Glioblastoma) terminal brain cancer. He was unsure of the ultimate timeline and treatment path, he told me, but he felt pretty sure his time would be short.

It sucked. Big time.

Still, in Dr. Friedland's true spirit, he decided to go for whatever successes he could still achieve: asking me to continue to receive coaching, and announcing that together with his family, they have launched a YouTube channel called "Living Well from Within." Here, they are sharing with as many other families as they can (from both home and work) an unfolding playlist, which you can binge watch (https://bit.ly/LivingWellFromWithin) as you would a Netflix series. This playlist serves as an ongoing real-life human drama filled with transformational lessons that facilitate healing, growth, and thriving in the lives of individuals, communities, and the world.

I encourage you to watch the magic that's been unfolding in this playlist. At this moment in time, Dr. Friedland wants to use whatever time he has remaining to build a movement of meaningful influence with this channel.

He wants to shine a light on all whom he has been blessed to have worked with that are doing the great work of facilitating, healing, growing, and flourishing to make a meaningful difference in the world. Essentially, he is building a coalition of healing influence that can benefit all whom are suffering in the world at this historic time of need and opportunity.

All I ask is that if you feel inspired to join this coalition of healing influence, simply subscribe to this channel. If you feel moved to bless others in your network with this purposeful playlist, please share this as widely as you can with an encouragement for all others in your networks to subscribe to this channel, too.

Dr. Friedland shared with me that his highest wish for you would be to ask yourself in any moment of adversity, What matters most now? For Dr. Friedland, the answer he received the first evening after receiving his diagnosis, lying alone in his hospital bed, was to "make every moment count!" The question that naturally followed next was, How? The answers that followed were to live with greater intention in the cycle of receiving and giving love in every touchpoint of relationship, and to take action to elevate the purpose of his life's work. This led him to establish his Living Well from Within YouTube channel, from which we can now all benefit.

Extraordinary.

I was so moved by his loving energy and his desire to continue to impact the world, to give and receive love, I was in tears for nearly all of our forty-five-minute call.

So, to Dr. Daniel Friedland. You are the perfect teacher for my life's journey. You have helped me grow more as a man, a father, a leader, and a coach more than anyone I have ever met. You are the guide of my Life by Design Journey, and your teachings have changed my life in the best ways possible. You are a huge piece of the heart and soul of this book.

References

1. Bob Anderson, *The Leadership Circle and Organizational Performance (The Leadership Circle, n.d.)*, http://ourleadershipmatters.com/wp-content/uploads/2016/02/The-Leadership-Circle-and-Organizational-Performance.pdf.

2. David A. Kolb, *Experiential Learning: Experience as the Source of Learning and Development*, 2nd ed. (Upper Saddle River, NJ: Pearson Education, 2015).

3. Gabriele Oettingen, *Rethinking Positive Thinking: Inside the New Science of Motivation*, (New York: Current, 2015).

4. Dan Sullivan, "What Is the Ceiling of Complexity?", *Strategic Coach*, accessed October 17, 2020, https://resources.strategiccoach.com/the-multiplier-mindset-blog/what-is-the-ceiling-of-complexity.

5. Dan Sullivan, "What Is the Ceiling of Complexity?"

6. Daniel Friedland, *Leading Well from Within: A Neuroscience and Mindfulness-Based Framework for Conscious Leadership* (San Diego: SuperSmartHealth, 2016).

7. Daniel Friedland, *Leading Well from Within.*

8. Daniel Friedland, *Leading Well from Within.*

9. Daniel Friedland, *Leading Well from Within.*

10. Jim Collins, *Good to Great: Why Some Companies Make the Leap . . . and Others Don't*, (New York: HarperCollins, 2001).

11. Jim Collins, *Good to Great*.

12. *Entrepreneur.com*. https://www.entrepreneur.com/article/243054

13. Brian Scudamore, *WTF?! (Willing to Fail): How Failure Can Be Your Key to Success*, (Lioncrest Publishing, 2018).

14. Brené Brown, *Dare to Lead: Brave Work. Tough Conversations. Whole Hearts,* (New York: Random House, 2018).

15. Jim Collins, *Good to Great*.

16. Mark Manson, *The Subtle Art of Not Giving a F*ck,* (New York: HarperOne, 2016).

17. Mark Manson, *The Subtle Art of Not Giving a F*ck*.

18. Mark Manson, *The Subtle Art of Not Giving a F*ck*.

19. Simon Sinek, *Start with Why: How Great Leaders Inspire Everyone to Take Action,* (New York: Penguin Group, 2009).

20. Simon Sinek, *Start with Why*.

21. Hector Garcia and Francese Miralles, *Ikigai: The Japanese Secret to a Long and Happy Life* (London: Penguin Life, 2017).

22. *Psychology Today*, "Fear," https://www.psychologytoday.com/us/basics/fear.

23. Megan Dalla-Camina, "The Reality of Imposter Syndrome," *Real Women* (blog), Psychology Today, September 3, 2018, https://www.psychologytoday.com/us/blog/real-women/201809/the-reality-imposter-syndrome.

24. Megan Dalla-Camina, "The Reality of Imposter Syndrome."

25. Megan Dalla-Camina, "The Reality of Imposter Syndrome."

26. Brené Brown, *Daring Greatly: How the Courage to Be Vulnerable Transforms the Way We Live, Love, Parent, and Lead,* (New York: Avery, 2012).

27. Brené Brown,, *Daring Greatly.*

28. Brené Brown,, *Daring Greatly.*

29. Jack Stack, *The Great Game of Business: The Only Sensible Way to Run a Company,* (New York: Crown Business, 1992).

30. Cameron Herold Facebook post. https://www.facebook.com/cameron.herold.77/posts/10164225687920297

31. Barbara Corcoran (@BarbaraCorcoran), Twitter, November 11, 2016, https://twitter.com/BarbaraCorcoran/status/797168401319862273.

32. Ron Howard, dir. *Apollo 13*, Beverly Hills, CA: Imagine Entertainment, 1995.

33. Ben Rueck, https://www.climbing.com/skills/ben-rueck-how-to-climb-out-of-your-comfort-zone/ 2016

34. Ben Rueck, *How to Climb Out of Your Comfort Zone.*

35. Ben Rueck, *How to Climb Out of Your Comfort Zone.*

36 .Ben Rueck, *How to Climb Out of Your Comfort Zone.*

37. Ben Rueck, *How to Climb Out of Your Comfort Zone.*

38. John Gall, *Systemantics: How Systems Work and Especially How They Fail* (New York: Quadrangle, 1977).

39. Deb Gabor, *Branding Is Sex: Get Your Customers Laid and Sell the Hell Out of Anything,* (Austin: Lioncrest, 2016).

40. Deb Gabor, *Branding Is Sex.*

41. Deb Gabor, *Branding Is Sex.*

42. Chris Krimitsos. *Start Ugly: A Timeless Tale about Innovation & Change,* (Tampa: Shake Creative, 2019).

44. Deb Gabor, *Branding Is Sex.*

45. Jordan Steen, "How I Made $300,000 by Giving Everything Away for FREE," *Cereal Entrepreneur,* October 13, 2018, https://cerealentrepreneur. academy/content-strategy-made-300000-giving-everything-away-free/.

46. Joe Pulizzi, *Content Inc.: How Entrepreneurs Use Content to Build Massive Audiences and Create Radically Successful Businesses,* (New York: McGraw-Hill Education, 2016).

47. Scott Adams, *How to Fail at Almost Everything and Still Win Big: Kind of the Story of My Life,* (New York: Portfolio/Penguin, 2013).

48. Scott Adams, *How to Fail at Almost Everything.*

49. Marissa Levin, "8 Ways to Build a Culture of Trust Based on Harvard's Neuroscience Research," *Inc.,* October 5, 2017, https://www.inc.com/marissa-levin/harvard-neuroscience-research-reveals-8-ways-to-build-a-culture-of-trust.html.

50. Levin, "8 Ways to Build a Culture of Trust."

51. Levin, "8 Ways to Build a Culture of Trust."

52. Levin, "8 Ways to Build a Culture of Trust."

53. Zeynep Ton, *The Good Jobs Strategy: How the Smartest Companies Invest in Employees to Lower Costs and Boost Profits,* (Boston: New Harvest, 2014).

54. Ton, *The Good Jobs Strategy.*